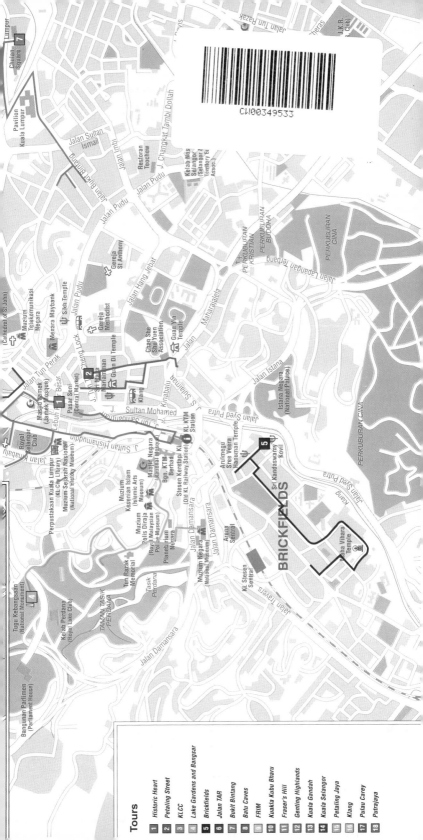

Tours

1. Historic Heart
2. Petaling Street
3. KLCC
4. Lake Gardens and Bangsar
5. Brickfields
6. Jalan TAR
7. Bukit Bintang
8. Batu Caves
9. FRIM
10. Kuala Kubu Bharu
11. Fraser's Hill
12. Genting Highlands
13. Kuala Gandah
14. Kuala Selangor
15. Petaling Jaya
16. Klang
17. Pulau Carey
18. Putrajaya

CW00349533

INSIGHT GUIDES

KUALA LUMPUR

Step by Step

DISCOVERY CHANNEL

APA PUBLICATIONS

Part of the Langenscheidt Publishing Group

CONTENTS

ABOUT THIS BOOK

Above from top: Sultan Abdul Samad Building; Central Market shops; cable car ride at Genting Highlands; Jalan Ampang shophouses; Malaysia's national flower at Hibiscus Garden.

This *Step by Step Guide* has been produced by the editors of Insight Guides, whose books have set the standard for visual travel guides since 1970. With top-quality photography and authoritative recommendations, this guidebook brings you the very best of Kuala Lumpur in a series of 18 tailor-made tours.

WALKS AND TOURS

The tours in the book provide something to suit all budgets, tastes and trip lengths. As well as covering Kuala Lumpur's classic attractions, of which there are myriad, the tours track lesser-known sights and up-and-coming areas; there are also longer excursions for those who want to extend their visit outside the bustling city.

The tours embrace a range of interests, so whether you are an art enthusiast, a gourmet, a park lover, an architecture buff or have kids in tow, you will find an option to suit.

We recommend that you read the whole of a tour before setting out. This should help you to familiarise yourself with the tour and enable you to plan where to stop for refreshments – options for this are shown in the 'Food and Drink' boxes, recognisable by the knife and fork sign.

For our pick of the walks by theme, consult Recommended Tours For… *(see pp.6–7)*.

OVERVIEW

The tours are placed in context by this introductory section, giving an overview of the city to set the scene, plus background information on food and drink, shopping and nightlife. A succinct history timeline in this chapter highlights the key events that have shaped Kuala Lumpur over the centuries.

DIRECTORY

Also supporting the tours is the Directory chapter, comprising a user-friendly, clearly organised A-Z of practical information, our pick of where to stay while you are in the city and select restaurant listings; these eateries complement the more low-key cafés and restaurants that feature within the tours themselves and are intended to offer a wider choice for evening dining.

The Author

SL Wong is a Malaysia-born freelance writer who has used Kuala Lumpur as her base for almost two decades. Having lived in Australia, Singapore and Hong Kong, she loves KL's eclectic blend of Asian chaos and globalised influences. Day and night, for work and for play, she thrives on the energy generated by the city's multifarious cultures, inherited traditions and its quirky charms. Besides the heavenly food, she finds escape from urban frenzy a short drive away in the charms of rural life and the restorative energy of primeval rainforests.

Margin Tips
Shopping tips, quirky anecdotes, historical facts and interesting snippets help visitors make the most of their time in Kuala Lumpur.

Feature Boxes
Notable topics are highlighted in these special boxes.

Key Facts Box
This box gives details of the distance covered on the tour, plus an estimate of how long it should take. It also states where the route starts and finishes, and gives key travel information such as which days are best to do the tour or handy transport tips.

Route Map
Detailed cartography with the walk or tour clearly plotted using numbered dots. For more detailed mapping, see the pull-out map, which is slotted inside the back cover.

Food and Drink
Recommendations of where to stop for refreshments are given in these boxes. The numbers prior to each café/restaurant name link to references in the main text. Places recommended en route are also plotted on the maps.

The $ signs given in each entry reflect the approximate cost of a three-course meal for one person without drinks. These should be seen as a guide only. Price ranges, which are also quoted on the inside back flap for easy reference, are as follows:

$$$$	over RM90
$$$	RM60–90
$$	RM30–60
$	below RM30

Footers
Those on the left-hand page usually give the tour name, plus, where relevant, a map reference; those on the right-hand page mostly cite the main sight on the double page.

ARCHITECTURE

The contemporary Petronas Twin Towers (walk 3) contrasts with the colonial Mughal-style Sultan Abdul Samad Building (walk 1), while tradition is preserved in the headman's house, Rumah Penghulu Abu Seman (walk 7) and nationhood celebrated in the National Museum (walk 4).

RECOMMENDED TOURS FOR...

ARTS BUFFS

Discover regional artefacts at the Museum of Asian Art (tour 15) and the Pucuk Rebung Royal Gallery-Museum (walk 3), while contemporary art can be perused at the Petronas Gallery (walk 3) and National Art Gallery (walk 6).

EXTREME SPORTS

Climb, slide and crawl through the Dark Caves in a spot of adventure caving (tour 8), experience weightlessness on the G-Force X (tour 15) or shoot rapids on the Selangor River (tour 10).

FAMILIES WITH KIDS

Petrosains makes the oil and gas industry – and science – a ton of fun (walk 3). Get close to Asian elephants at Kuala Gandah (tour 13). Theme park fans should head to Sunway Lagoon (tour 15) and the Genting Theme Park (tour 12).

FESTIVALS

Prayers, decorations and festive food dominate during festivals, such as the Muslim Hari Raya Aidilfitri in Kampung Baru (walk 6), Chinese New Year in Petaling Street and Bukit Bintang (walks 2 and 7), Wesak Day in Brickfields (walk 5) and the Hindu Thaipusam celebration in Batu Caves (walk 8).

FOOD AND DRINK

Sample Malaysians' favourite breakfast of *nasi lemak* (coconut rice) at Nasi Lemak Tanglin (walk 4), the KL speciality of Hokkien *mee* at Chinatown Seng Kee (walk 2), Ginger Restaurant's delectable Malay dry curry *rendang* (walk 1) and a great Indian vegetarian spread at Saravanaa Bhavan (walk 6).

NIGHTLIFE

Nightbirds will love the throbbing club action at Jalan P. Ramlee (walk 3) and Asian Heritage Row (walk 3), as well as the quieter Changkat Bukit Bintang watering holes (walk 7). For theatre, check out the Central Market annexe (walk 1) and for music, the Dewan Filharmonik Petronas (walk 3).

ESCAPING THE CROWDS

Escape the frenetic city pace; head to the leafy Lake Gardens or the fountain courtyard at the Islamic Arts Museum (walk 4). Find peace in the open spaces of the National Mosque (walk 1) and the secluded Guan Di Temple (walk 2).

SHOPPING

Shop for souvenirs at the Central Market (walk 1), Jalan Masjid India (walk 6) and Petaling Street (walk 2). Shopping centres not to be missed are the Mid Valley Megamall (walk 4) and Sungei Wang Plaza (walk 7).

RAINFOREST ENCOUNTERS

Amazing rainforest discoveries include lowland forest canopies at the Canopy Walkway (walk 9), riverine vegetation at Chiling Waterfall (tour 10), mangroves and mudflats at the Kuala Selangor Nature Park (tour 14) and misty montane habitats at Fraser's Hill (tour 11).

OVERVIEW

An introduction to Kuala Lumpur's geography, culture and people, plus illuminating background information on food and drink, shopping, nightlife and history.

CITY OVERVIEW

Kuala Lumpur was never the centre of an ancient civilisation. Yet in its short lifespan, it has become a major player in Southeast Asia, embracing globalisation yet retaining its distinctly multiethnic cadences.

Above: faces of multicultural KL.

Tin and Rubber
The Malay Peninsula supplied over half the world's tin in the early 1900s. Towards the end of the 19th century, the British introduced rubber, another successful commodity that turned large swathes of rainforest into plantations.

Right: efficient Monorail system.

Just 150 years ago, Kuala Lumpur – or KL, as it is popularly known – was nothing more than marsh, muck and mudbank. Today, it is a cosmopolitan fibre-optic-wired commercial centre, learned in the street smarts of the Western world and driven by capitalism and globalisation. Yet, the city is also steeped in the rich and variegated traditions of Malay, Chinese, Indian and other cultures. This multilayered persona is evident in everything from architecture and music to festivals and KL-ites' favourite preoccupation – food.

DEVELOPMENT

In 1857, an expedition of Chinese tin miners headed up the Klang River from Pengkalan Batu (now Port Klang). When they arrived at the confluence of the Klang and Gombak rivers, they had to stop as the rivers were too shallow to accommodate their fully laden flotilla. Their resting place was nothing more than a tiny hamlet nestled in a quagmire of mud. Appropriately, the miners called the settlement Kuala Lumpur – meaning 'muddy confluence'.

Tin was eventually found in Ampang, upstream of KL, but because the rivers were too shallow, KL remained a convenient staging point for supplies and ore. Buoyed by high tin prices, the settlement developed into a booming mining town by the 1860s.

19th Century

The miners were Chinese immigrants who came under community leaders called the 'Kapitan Cina'. The most illustrious was Yap Ah Loy, a Hakka immigrant, who rebuilt KL at least

three times, once after the Selangor Civil War and twice after the great fire of 1881, and governed it like his own little kingdom until the first British Resident (ruler) turned up in 1880.

The next major personality was Frank Swettenham, the Resident of Selangor appointed in 1882. Together with Yap, he replaced the shanties and huts that formed much of KL with brick structures, and constructed the KL–Klang railway link, ending the city's dependence on the river.

An active policy of emigration and the encouragement of agriculture on its periphery increased the Malay and Indian populations while diminishing the economic control wielded by Chinese migrants. In 1896 KL was declared capital of the Federated Malay States. Both world wars did little damage to the city, and in 1963, KL became the capital of Malaysia. The city was declared a Federal Territory in 1974. Since then, KL has bloomed into one of the most modern cities in Southeast Asia.

MODERN KUALA LUMPUR

In the 1990s, KL became the site for a building boom of massive skyscrapers, which are symbols of Malaysia's aspirations to gain developed nation status. The most significant are the Petronas Twin Towers. These and other national mega projects, a good selection of which are found in the capital, are funded largely by foreign loans, something that has not been overly helpful to the country's debt levels.

KL's impressive modern structures do give it an international feel. Some visitors like this, since they can find enough global stamps of familiarity to be able to take to the city easily. However, in some areas, basic infrastructure has not kept pace with the city's unbridled growth. The traffic jams, pollution and crowded streets are evidence of this.

There are, however, pockets of the old KL still evident. So you may come across a colourful Hindu temple at a busy junction, or a row of pre-war shophouses behind a ritzy mall, while the sound of squawking chickens could lead you to a fresh-produce market that has existed for generations.

ORIENTATION

KL is situated about halfway down the west coast of the peninsula and 35km

Above from far left: colonial architecture; the symbols of modern KL; Sin Sze Si Ya Temple at Petaling Street.

Tourist-Friendly
Spruced up for Visit Malaysia 2007, KL is tourist-friendly, with a slew of hospitality facilities and services. Attractions are well sign-posted and in English. The service industry is a key economic activity in the city.

Below: skyscrapers line KL's cityscape.

Parklands

KL is surprisingly green. Occupying prime land is the Bukit Nanas Forest Reserve around the Menara KL, and the manicured Lake Gardens southwest of the old city centre.

Below: woman in traditional *tudung* (headscarf).

(22 miles) inland. It is bordered on the east by the Titiwangsa mountains and sits in the Klang river basin. A metropolis with an area of about 234sq km (90sq miles), KL anchors a conurbation known as the Klang Valley, which roughly follows the Klang River that empties into the Straits of Malacca. The Klang Valley encompasses cities like Petaling Jaya, Shah Alam and Klang, and the federal administrative capital of Putrajaya.

Right in the old heart of KL is the colonial core around the Padang, where the Europeans used to hang out; the new heart east of that is the KL City Centre (KLCC), home to the Petronas Twin Towers. Next to the old heart is Petaling Street and, in the north, Jalan Tuanku Abdul Rahman leads to Kampung Baru. South of the KLCC is the shopping and commercial centre of Bukit Bintang, which sits in the financial and commercial area known as the Golden Triangle.

Navigating the City

Most attractions are accessible on foot, although pedestrian walkways were obviously not a top priority on the town builders' agendas. Heavy traffic and pollution do not help. Nonetheless, walking is the quickest way to get around during the gridlock rush hours of 7–9am and 4–7pm on weekdays.

To travel between attractions, take the air-conditioned Light Rail Transport System (LRT), Monorail or KTM Komuter electric trains. A network of trains and buses also takes you to attractions outside of the city centre. Alternatively, taxis are cheap, so book one for the day. Many of the attractions covered in this guide are also part of guided bus tours from KL.

A MELTING POT

KL has the country's highest per capita GDP and an employment-to-population ratio twice that of other metropolitan areas. Its population of over 1.4 million swells to 2.5 million in the daytime when workers commute from the Klang Valley. A large migrant labour force plays an indispensable role in its economy. KL-ites tend to manifest many of the traits of an urbanised population. They have a more international outlook compared to residents in the rest of the country and tend to be better travelled and are more influenced by global trends.

Large numbers of Chinese started settling in KL in the 19th century, eventually dominating commerce. Today, they make up 40 percent of KL's

population. Malays, too, make up 40 percent; large numbers migrated from the rural areas in the 1970s–80s for economic reasons. Most work in the service and government sectors. About 5 percent of KL-ites are Indians who arrived as manual labourers, mainly from South India, but a fair sprinkling of Northerners, notably Punjabis, Sikhs and Gujeratis, came to KL for business.

While core ethnic values are largely preserved, especially in religion and marriage, borrowings and adaptations are rampant and imaginative in everything from language and dress to food and social mores. Growing affluence and the common pursuit of material gains also tend to level out differences. On any given street, you will see Chinese and Malay businessmen in shirtsleeves and ties sweat over a curry lunch at an Indian Muslim restaurant. At weekends nightclubs are filled with trendy 20- and 30-somethings dancing to R&B or Latin grooves, even while some in the group might abstain from alcohol or beef for religious purposes.

A TRADITIONAL SPIRIT

All Malays are Muslim. Constitutionally, Islam is Malaysia's designated official religion, though freedom of religion is assured for the other races. The main religions practised are Islam, Buddhism, Taoism and Christianity. Places of worship of different faiths co-exist while cultural and religious festivals are celebrated freely. Malaysia projects an image of a moderate Muslim nation in a troubled post-9/11 world, although

maintaining a harmonious balance has always been challenging.

Etiquette

Some social and religious norms apply to only one community, others to all. It is polite, for instance, to remove your shoes before entering the homes of any Malaysian. Pointing your foot or finger at anybody is considered insulting. Proper behaviour and attire (covered arms and legs) is expected of everyone in all places of worship. When you are in doubt about what is right or wrong, ask. Most KL-ites are friendly and will not hesitate to help visitors to their city.

Above from far left: blooms in a KL park; busy Bukit Bintang; Zion Cathedral in Brickfields.

Malays
Malays are culturally a mix of Javanese, Sumatran, Siamese and Indian. All Malays are Muslim; to renounce Islam is a crime punishable by law.

Multicultural Celebrations

Probably one of the most delightful aspects of KL's multiculturalism is the 'open house'. This is when people from different ethnic backgrounds visit one another during the respective cultural celebrations. Celebrants open their houses to friends and neighbours of all faiths all day long during the festive period, and there is always food on hand regardless of whether it is mealtime. These festive periods are also when the city folk discard their usual Western-style clothing for more traditional ethnic or ethnic-inspired garb.

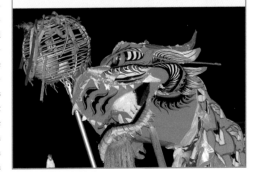

FOOD AND DRINK

KL is probably not the best place to be on a diet. The variety is endless, the portions large and the prices reasonable. Choose from Malay, Chinese, Indian and Nonya food, as well as international cuisines and fusion fare.

Above: grilled chicken wings and rice on banana leaf are just some of Malaysia's favourite local treats.

Peranakans
The community has its roots in the 15th century, when migrant Chinese men who settled in Penang, Melaka and Singapore married local women; over the years, their descendants assimilated many local Malay customs, fashioning a unique fusion culture of their own.

Drawn by the economic magnet of KL, Malaysians from all over the country have settled in the city, bringing with them cuisines of their own. Regional specialities are easily available, but so are innovations. These include 'beef bacon' to meet *halal* needs, Chinese-style stir-fried vegetables on an Indian menu, and contemporary Asian fare featuring a touch of the European. Beer is available in most non-Muslim eateries, and wine is increasingly available in the fancier restaurants.

MALAY CUISINE

A cornucopia of herbs and spices such as lemon grass, *galangal* and turmeric imparts a heady bouquet to Malay food. *Nasi lemak*, rice cooked in coconut milk and served with condiments like peanuts, fried anchovies, cucumber and *sambal* chilli, is a breakfast favourite. Another popular treat is *satay*: skewers of marinated meat charcoal-grilled and served with peanut sauce and rice cakes.

The mainstay is the meal of plain white rice accompanied by side dishes such as *rendang*, a dry beef curry; *sambal goreng*, long beans fried with chilli paste and bean curd; and *kangkung* (water spinach) stir-fried with *belacan* (shrimp paste).

Malay food has its share of regional innovations. Food from the east coast tends to be sweeter, while that from the south has Arabic influences, whereas northern food hints of Thai accents.

CHINESE CUISINE

Malaysia's Chinese immigrants hail from the southern provinces of China, and today belong to such dialect groups as the Cantonese, Hokkiens, Hainanese, Hakkas and Teochews.

From the Cantonese come favourites such as *char siu* (barbecued pork), dim sum and a refined banquet cuisine known for its delicate flavours. Representative of Hokkien street food is Hokkien *mee*, thick yellow wheat noodles fried in soy sauce with pork, prawns and squid. Another Hokkien dish is *bak kut teh*, a soup of herbs and pork ribs. Teochews are most famous for their plain rice gruel eaten with salty, preserved food, as well as richer fare like braised goose and creamy yam custard.

Hakkas originated *yeung dau fu*, an assortment of bean curd and vegetables stuffed with fish and meat paste. Many Hainanese immigrants worked as cooks for the British, and from them come Chinese-influenced 'Western' dishes such as chicken chop with Worcestershire sauce.

NONYA CUISINE

Nonya, or Peranakan, food is similar to Malay food but has decidedly Chinese twists. Complex spice pastes are painstakingly pounded by hand, and *kuih*, or sweet confections, are very time-consuming to prepare. Standards include *lemak nanas* (pineapple curry) or *kuah lada* (pepper curry), which are more Malay in character, while dishes like *pongteh*, a salty-sweet gravy redolent of soy bean paste, are more Chinese.

INDIAN CUISINE

The early Indian immigrants came mainly from South India. They brought with them griddle-cooked breads like *roti canai* and *thosai*, spicy curries, and the tradition of using the hand to eat food heaped on banana leaves.

In the earlier years, Indian Muslim hawkers would carry rice *(nasi)* and curry in two baskets balanced on a *kandar*, or pole, to cater to labourers. This is how the curry-focused *nasi kandar* cuisine came about; it can now be found in just about every coffee shop.

The mainstays of North Indian cuisine are tandoori chicken and naan, now available even in casual eateries, while the finer dishes of the maharajahs are served in sumptuously appointed restaurants.

WHERE TO EAT

The gradual sophistication of the city's palate has spawned a new breed of cafés, bistros and fine-dining restaurants offering European and Asian cuisines. But the unassuming stars of the dining scene are still the hawker stalls and coffee shops serving humble local specialities.

Open-Air Dining

Supper is KL-ites' favourite end to an evening, with many thronging hawker stalls and *mamak* eateries (Indian Muslim stalls) late at night. These offer lots of local colour and everything from Indian *roti canai* to fried Chinese-style noodles, to a glass of *teh tarik* (literally, 'pulled tea', a frothy tea concoction).

Open-air hawker centres are located all over the city and some of the larger ones are in Petaling Street (Chinese food); Jalan Alor (mostly Chinese); Kampung Baru (mostly Malay food); Jalan Imbi (Chinese); and Lucky Garden in Bangsar (Indian).

Some hawkers keep going till 2 or 3am and there are others who even keep their stalls open till dawn, such as the ubiquitous 24-hour *mamak* joints.

Above from far left: roast meats at a coffee shop; Indian sweets; Chinese-style curry noodles.

Seafood and Vegetarian Cuisine
Seafood is a Malaysian favourite, done Chinese or Malay style, while vegetarian food has both Chinese and Indian varieties.

Below: open-air dining on Jalan Alor.

SHOPPING

At first glance, it may seem that KL's retail scene is all about designer boutiques and ritzy malls. But there are also crafts and cultural finds, street markets and ethnic neighbourhoods, which appeal to all kinds of shoppers.

Bargaining
Although the law requires retail outlets to affix price tags on all goods sold, bargaining is still an integral part of the Malaysian shopping experience, so you should be prepared to haggle. The exception is in department stores and boutiques, where prices are fixed.

Books
The major retailers for English-language books are Times and MPH and have chains in malls. Kinokuniya, in Suria KLCC, is Malaysia's biggest bookstore. For Malaysiana, head to Silverfish Books (www.silverfishbooks.com) in Bangsar.

With its numerous luxurious malls and stylish designer boutiques, KL is a veritable shopper's paradise, on a par with Asian cities like Singapore, Hong Kong and Bangkok. At the same time, it also offers some good opportunities for craft collectors and bargain hunters in its craft galleries and street markets.

SHOPPING MALLS

For better quality and designer labels, the best bets are the large shopping complexes. The **Bukit Bintang** area is the city's undisputed consumer hub, with a gamut of retail offerings from luxurious goods in **Starhill Gallery** and **Pavilion Kuala Lumpur** *(see p.61)* to funky, affordable streetwear in **Sungei Wang Plaza** *(see p.62)* and **Bukit Bintang Plaza**.

Many shopping centres in KL are worlds unto their own. Other than boutiques and department stores, they come complete with cineplexes, restaurants and hypermarkets. Fine examples of these include **Suria KLCC** *(see p.39)* at the base of the Petronas Twin Towers and **Mid Valley Megamall** *(see p.49)* in the city's outskirts. Further afield from the city centre, air-conditioned retail options that make worthwhile excursions include the **Bangsar Shopping Centre** and

Bangsar Village *(see p.49)* in Bangsar, and **1 Utama**, **The Curve** and **Sunway Pyramid** *(see p.86)* in Petaling Jaya.

MARKETS

Despite the profusion of mega malls in the city, traditional markets still have their loyal clientele, and are colourful repositories of activity, sounds and smells. Fresh-produce markets generally operate from 5am until noon. The city's largest wet market is the **Chow Kit Market** *(see p.56)* in Jalan Tuanku Abdul Rahman, while one of the oldest is the **Petaling Street Market** *(see p.34)*.

Night Markets

The more accessible and fun *pasar malam*, or night markets, are usually set up around 6pm. Some *pasar malam* are itinerant, so check with your hotel or the City Hall (www.dbkl.com.my). Mingle with the locals as they haggle over fresh produce, cheap clothing and toys and household goods; sample local snacks or hawker food. Worth visiting are the *pasar malam* along **Jalan Telawi Satu** in Bangsar (Sunday); along **Lorong Tuanku Abdul Rahman** (Saturday) in the Masjid India area; and along **Jalan Berhala** in Brickfields (Thursday). The most famous *pasar*

malam in KL is the **Petaling Street Bazaar** *(see p.34)*, which has become an institution in its own right.

Flea Markets

The most popular weekend bazaar is the **Amcorp Mall Flea Market**, which has an assortment of old records, books, antiques and toys. Higher-end flea markets are found in Sri Hartamas and Bangsar, where stalls sell fashion, jewellery and home-made cookies. Culture and shopping are combined at the Istana Budaya's (National Theatre) **Laman Santai**, an art market held every Saturday night with works and performances by local artists *(see p.56)*.

HANDICRAFTS

Move away from the big brands in contemporary malls and you will discover the cultural side of KL's shopping landscape.

Traditional Fabrics

Handed down from the grand courts of Kelantan in the Peninsula's east coast, *songket* fabric is a display of dramatic handwoven tradition featuring intricate tapestry inlaid with gold and metallic threads. Its richness makes it more suitable as formal and ceremonial attire. The rich fabric is also frequently made into formal jackets, evening wear and handbags and shoes.

Batik, the less glamorous cousin of *songket*, has more appeal because of its versatility, durability and lower price. Also originally from the east coast, batik is now printed by factories all over the country, on fabrics ranging from cotton and voile to silk and satin. It is used for clothes, accessories, household and decorative items.

Silvercraft and Pewterware

Kelantan silvercraft is one of the most successful cottage industries in Malaysia. It is a craft requiring a great amount of skill, whether in filigree work, where ornamental wire is shaped into delicate tracery, or repousses, where sheet silver is hammered into patterned relief. Kelantan silver is fashioned into a variety of items, from brooches and costume jewellery to serving dishes and tableware.

KL's own local handicraft, Royal Selangor pewterware, enjoys a worldwide reputation for its stylish and

Above from far left: international boutique at Suria KLCC; Vincci is a popular local shoe brand; browsing for handicrafts at Central Market.

Below: Malay *songket* made into formal traditional wear.

**Electronics and
IT Products**
Cameras, computers
and IT equipment are
relatively inexpensive
as they are duty free.
A wide variety of
these items are avail-
able, and retail outlets
can be found in
shopping malls.
Dedicated IT malls
are Plaza Low Yat
and Imbi Plaza
in Bukit Bintang.

Below: batik art.

attractive handmade designs. Pewter is an alloy of tin mixed with a little copper and antimony and was introduced to Malaysia from China in the 18th century. The hardness of the metal gives it durability, and its silvery finish does not tarnish. Using traditional methods of casting and soldering, hundreds of items ranging from tableware, candelabra and ornamental pieces to lapel pins, figurines and pendants are crafted.

Kites and Tops

The traditional *wau* (kites) and *gasing* (tops), for which the Peninsula's east coast is best known, enjoy both local and international popularity. Both are traditional sports, with kite flying dating to as far back as the 14th century.

The *wau* comes in all shapes and sizes. The most popular and the largest is the *wau bulan* or moon kite, measuring 3½m (11½ft) from head to tail and capable of soaring to great heights.

Its wooden frame is covered with stiff parchment decorated with designs cut from coloured paper and adorned with colourful streamers. Smaller versions are made as decorative items.

Top spinning is no child's play either, not when the traditional Malay top is about the size of a dinner plate and weighs as much as 5½kg (12lbs). The tops are usually disc shaped, and are carefully balanced for spinning power.

Bamboo Products and Beadwork

Cane and wicker are used for furniture and household items. *Mengkuang* (pandanus) leaves are woven into mats, baskets, hats and decorative items, and split bamboo strips are shaped into trays, baskets and household items.

Beadwork, native to Sabah and Sarawak, is extremely attractive when sewn onto headbands, necklaces, belts, buttons and baskets. Those available for sale in KL tend to be commercial, but still make for attractive souvenirs – at least the designs are native.

Much rarer is the intricate beadwork from the Melaka Peranakan heritage, a blend of Malay and Chinese cultures. This finely crafted work appears on embroidered evening handbags and slippers (*manik-manik*), and feature in select local haute couture labels.

Where to Buy

The best Malaysian handicrafts, unfortunately, are not found in KL, but in their home states. A good variety, however, can be found in the **Kompleks Kraf Kuala Lumpur**, **Suria KLCC**, **Peter Hoe Beyond** (Petaling

Street area) and the **Central Market**. Pewter gifts and homeware can be purchased in department stores and from Royal Selangor boutiques in Setapak Jaya and major malls.

Aseana and **Pucuk Rebung**, both at Suria KLCC, are delightful emporiums of Asian- and Malaysian-inspired gifts, fashion, fabrics and handicrafts.

Jalan Masjid India and **Jalan Tuanku Abdul Rahman** are good places to shop for traditional fabrics.

FASHION

Malaysia is a prolific producer of textiles and apparel, so there is no shortage of good-quality cotton, linen and silk items. Most department stores carry selections of local and international brands. Most outfits are best suited to warm, tropical climates, and large sizes can sometimes be difficult to find. However, tailors are equipped to handle made-to-measure orders at fairly reasonable prices and can sometimes deliver within 24 hours.

KL has all the international designer labels for the brand-conscious, but the truly great buys are Malaysian-designed fashion brands. **Vincci** is a chain that does trendy, affordable women's shoes and accessories, while **Padini** and **Seed** carry both reasonably priced basics and seasonal discounts. **British India** is more upmarket, with ethnic home furnishings and well-designed clothes of natural fabrics for the whole family. **Zang Toi Collection** in Lot 10 carries the lower-priced diffusion lines, while **Salabianca** has

fashion on the glamorous side. **Aseana** in KLCC showcases the fashion of local designers including Melinda Looi, who crafts contemporary heritage-influenced haute couture, as well as handmade clothes from around Southeast Asia.

Above from far left: window display at the boutique of Malaysian designer Khoon Hui; Peranakan *kebaya*; local boutique.

Ethnic Fashion

The delicate Peranakan *kebaya* best represents the fusion of cultures in Malaysia, having evolved since the 16th century with European and Chinese influences. Unlike the long and voluminous Malay-style *baju kurung*, the *kebaya* is hip-length, form-fitting and often made with semi-transparent materials such as voile, silk and muslin. Exquisitely embroidered front panels, often with floral designs, are its characteristic feature. Fine needlework is one way of distinguishing a well-made *kebaya*, while status is also associated with the *kerosang*, linked gold brooches used to fasten the blouse. More likely worn on formal or festive occasions, the *kebaya* had once faded away with modernisation but has seen a recent revival, and both modern and traditional pieces are easily available. Other local traditional dress include the Chinese *cheongsam* and the Indian sari or *salwa khameez* trouser-suit. For men, there is the *baju Melayu*, a cotton or silk outfit with a mandarin collar and *sampin*, a sarong worn around the hips, and the Indian *khurta* cotton top.

NIGHTLIFE

Night-time KL without the daytime frenzy is gentler, its grime obscured and its contours delightfully lit. Whether it is eating, shopping, clubbing or pub crawling, there is enough to keep you awake till the wee hours.

Information
Besides newspapers, event listings can be found in magazines including *Faces* (www.faces.com.my), *Juice* (www.juice online.com) and *VisionKL* (www. visionkl.com).
The best online source of information for the arts is *Kakiseni* (www.kakiseni.com).

As darkness descends on KL, many KL-ites unwind and partake in their favourite after-sundown activities – eating out, partying and taking it easy. Most of the big hotels have their own bars; outside hotels, nightspots are clustered in entertainment areas such as Jalan P. Ramlee, Bukit Bintang and Asian Heritage Row in downtown KL, as well as in the suburban enclaves of Bangsar, Desa Sri Hartamas and Mutiara Damansara.

and **Beach Club** on **Jalan P. Ramlee** *(see p.43)*; each of these complexes comprises several restaurants and bars and has several dance areas. Nearby on **Jalan Ampang** is the ultra-hip **Zouk**. The swanky **Asian Heritage Row** *(see p.43)* in the Jalan Doraisamy area reigns as the place to be, with establishments like **Upstairs@The Loft**, **Cynna@The Loft** and **Maison**. Hotel hotspots include the **Latin Qba** at The Westin and Hilton Kuala Lumpur's **Zeta Bar**.

CLUBS

KL's clubbing scene is among the best in the region, with sophisticated venues, international DJs and a wide range of music choices. Clubbers tend to dress up, and some of the classier places have a 'no t-shirt, shorts or sandals' rule.

Most clubs are open 5pm–1am, with Happy Hours from 5.30–9pm. Generally, crowds swell after 11pm. Drinks are at half price during Happy Hours, which should be taken advantage of since alcohol is expensive in Malaysia. On weekends, the club scene rocks till 3am or later. Wednesday is ladies' night at most clubs, which means free drinks for the fairer sex.

The city nightspots tend to be big and glamorous; established 'institutions' include **Modesto's**, **Espanada**, **Nouvo**

PUBS AND BARS

Wines have become very popular, and a wide range is available, especially at wine and cigar bars. The Asian Heritage Row's glamorous hang-outs include **Bar Blonde**, **Bar Savanh** and **BED**. **Poppy Collection** *(see p.43)*, on Jalan P. Ramlee, has several sexy bars, but for unbeatable views, go to **Luna Bar** *(see p.43)* at the Pacific Regency Hotel Apartments.

Bukit Bintang's swish offerings include **Shook!** and **The Village Bar**, both in Starhill Gallery *(see p.61)*, while the atmospheric **Changkat Bukit Bintang** *(see p.63)* has plenty of choices, from **The Green Man** at the start of the strip to **Little Havana** at the far end.

Bangsar Baru *(see p.49)* is now a little jaded but regulars remain loyal to estab-

lishments like **Canteena's**, **Ronnie Q's**, **Alexis** and **Finnegan's**. In **Desa Sri Hartamas**, **Souled Out**, with an outdoor beer garden, is popular, as are the **Backyard Pub** and **Karma Hartamas**.

LIVE MUSIC

Live performances start late, usually around 10pm or 11pm, and there is normally a cover charge. Rock fans should head to **Hard Rock Café** at the Concorde Hotel and **Planet Hollywood** in Bukit Bintang.

Hotel Lounges

The entertainment in hotel lounges usually comprises easy listening music by a live band or a singer and pianist. One of the liveliest lounges is at the **Concorde Hotel** in Jalan Sultan Ismail; one of the poshest is at the **Hilton Kuala Lumpur** in KL Sentral.

Underground Music

The underground music scene largely comprises rock musicians writing and playing a wide range of sub-genres including punk, experimental and post-grunge. They perform in venues such as the **Central Market**'s annexe and the **Laundry Bar** at the Curve in Damansara Mutiara.

Jazz

Live jazz is played at establishments such as **Alexis Ampang** at Great Eastern Mall, **Groove Junction** in Desa Sri Hartamas, **Bangkok Jazz** in Chulan Square, and **Yoko's** in Changkat Bukit Bintang. **No Black Tie** on

Jalan Mesui, near Changkat Bukit Bintang, has a space for local musicians and songwriters, and continues to support budding jazz acts and Western classical musicians.

Classical Music

The top classical concert venue is the **Dewan Filharmonik Petronas** *(see p.43)* in Petronas Twin Towers. The concert hall presents a full programme by the Malaysian Philharmonic Orchestra and international musicians.

THEATRE AND DANCE

There is a small but active theatre and dance scene in KL. Of note are innovative intercultural works that engage both Asian and Western forms to showcase traditional aspects of Malaysia life in startling and new ways. The most important venues include the award-winning **Kuala Lumpur Performing Arts Centre** in Sentul, **Actor's Studio Theatre** in Bangsar Shopping Centre, **Panggung Bandaraya** on Jalan Raja, and **Istana Budaya** (National Theatre) on Jalan Tun Razak.

Above from far left: Luna Bar; Zouk; Shook! in Starhill Gallery; jazz performance.

Gay Scene
Nightlife choices are plentiful for the gay community. These include eateries, spas, saunas and clubs such as Blue Boy, Frangipani and Liquid. Straight clubs also hold regular gay and/or lesbian nights.

Below: Kuala Lumpur Performing Arts Centre.

HISTORY: KEY DATES

Kuala Lumpur was a remote mining town that grew to become Malaysia's capital. For a long time it played second fiddle to other Southeast Asian capitals; in the 'can-do' era of the 1990s, the city finally came of age.

EARLY HISTORY

AD700–1400	The peninsula comes under the control of the Southeast Asian Hindu empire known as Srivijaya.
*c.*1400	The port and sultanate of Melaka, the first great maritime power on the peninsula, is founded. Islam, first brought by traders and missionaries, becomes the state religion in 1446.

THE BIRTH OF KUALA LUMPUR

Kapitan Cina
Only 17 when he arrived in Malaya, Yap Ah Loy was the 'Chinese Captain' and is considered the founder of KL. He contributed significantly to the city's growth and rebuilt KL at least thrice after it was destroyed on various occasions. Of Yap's personality, a Chinese accountant once said, 'His temper was like fire and he had the strength of an elephant'. Today, a road is named after him, although it is only a mere 80m (262ft) long.

1857	KL is founded by tin miners and becomes a staging point for the trading of tin. Chinese labour is imported.
1867	Selangor is torn by civil war over the imposition of export duties on tin ore. War spreads to KL; in 1872, the settlement is razed.
1868–85	Yap Ah Loy is KL's 'Kapitan Cina' and develops the town.

BRITISH MALAYA

1882	Frank Swettenham is appointed Resident of Selangor.
1895	The Federated Malay States are formed.
1896	KL is declared capital of the Federated Malay States by the British.
1941–5	Japanese occupy the Malay Peninsula; British regain control after World War II.
1946	Rise of Malay nationalism. United Malays National Organisation (UMNO) is formed on 1 March.
1948	The Federation of Malaya is created, bringing together all peninsular states under British rule. The guerilla insurgency by the Malayan Communist Party leads to a State of Emergency.
1951	The Malayan Chinese Association (MCA) partners UMNO.
1953	The Malayan Indian Congress (MIC) joins the UMNO–MCA partnership, forming the Barisan Nasional (Alliance), which plays a major role in the country's independence struggle.
1955	Malaya's first national election; the Alliance wins 80 percent of votes.
1957	31 August: Malaya becomes an independent nation, with Tunku Abdul Rahman as prime minister. KL is made the capital of Malaya.

POST-INDEPENDENCE

Above from far left:
Selangor royalty;
UMNO flag.

1960	The State of Emergency is declared over.
1963	Singapore, Sabah and Sarawak join Malaya to form Malaysia.
1965	Singapore withdraws from Malaysia to become a republic.
1968	Politically motivated civil unrest breaks out between the Malays and Chinese.
1970	Tun Abdul Razak is appointed as Malaysia's second prime minister. The New Economic Policy is introduced, with affirmative action rights for *Bumiputra* (ethnic Malays and indigenous tribal people).
1972	KL is accorded city status.
1974	KL is annexed from Selangor to become a Federal Territory.
1975	Tun Hussein Onn takes over as prime minister.
1981	Tun Dr Mahathir Mohamad is appointed prime minister.
1986	The Proton Saga, the first locally manufactured car, is rolled out.
1991	The policy, Vision 2020, aims to make Malaysia a developed nation by 2020; Malaysia enjoys double-digit economic growth till 1997.
1996	The Petronas Twin Towers, then the world's tallest buildings, are completed. Multimedia Supercorridor, Malaysia's Silicon Valley, is launched.
1998	Kuala Lumpur International Airport opens. The economy takes a tumble, and currency controls are imposed.
1999	The Federal government's administrative offices move to Putrajaya; KL is now legislative capital, as well as financial and commercial centre.
2003	Datuk Seri Abdullah Ahmad Badawi is the fifth prime minister.
2004	KL Structure Plan 2020, focusing on urban growth and development, is gazetted.
2007	Street demonstrations show public dissatisfaction with the ruling party's administration and policies.
2008	Opposition parties do well at the polls, winning four state seats.

Left: on 31 August Malaysian flags are waved in celebration of the nation's independence, gained in 1957.

WALKS AND TOURS

HISTORIC HEART

Kuala Lumpur's original settlement began at the confluence of the Klang and Gombak rivers. Today, the centuries-old colonial buildings, minarets, spires and arches of the area continue to be sights that bewitch.

Vice Square
In the late 19th century, the original Market Square was a den of iniquity. Tin miners pursued their pastimes of gambling and opium smoking and pleasures of the flesh. The square was named after the Central Market, which was later moved to its current location.

This tour first leads you around the colonial administrative centre, which has a cluster of graceful Mughal-style buildings encircling a town field. The walk then takes you through more contemporary surroundings to another pair of magnificent Mughal-style edifices owned by the National Railways. End the day at the Central Market, a cultural attraction and souvenir marketplace.

MEDAN PASAR LAMA

There is no signage that indicates the location of the **Medan Pasar Lama ❶** (Old Market Square), as the original demarcations have disappeared due to urban renewal. Now roughly bordered by the streets of Lebuh Pasar Besar and Medan Pasar, the square was

originally the business and social centre of the early mining settlement, with a bustling market, brothels, and gambling and opium dens, housed in buildings made of wood and attap. The wooden huts were destroyed in the great fire of 1881, and the city's first brick houses were then built to replace them, under the governance of British Resident Frank Swettenham and local Chinese leader Yap Ah Loy. These were later demolished to make way for the double- and three-storey shophouses that now typify the architecture of the area.

Shophouses
These shophouses typically extend 30–60m/yd to the back, with the ground floor used for business, usually a shop; upstairs was where the proprietor's family lived. The newer three-storey shophouses were built in 1906–7 and they incorporated Western decorative details like fluted pilasters and ornate arched window frames and fanlights.

Today, only about half the shophouses have retained their original facades, each one different from its neighbour's. Housed in one of them on the left corner of Lebuh Pasar Besar and Medan Pasar is the traditional *kopitiam* (coffee shop) **Sin Seng Nam Restaurant**, see ⑪①, a good spot for breakfast.

Above from left:
shophouses of Medan Pasar Lama; clock tower; Jamek Mosque; Art Deco Oriental Building.

Clock Tower

After breakfast, walk to the **clock tower** opposite, towards the left. An Art Deco period piece with a signature sunburst motif, it was built in 1937 to commemorate the coronation of England's King George VI.

JAMEK MOSQUE

Continue on Medan Pasar till you come to a forked road. Take the left and you are now on Jalan Benteng. On your left you can clearly see the confluence of the Gombak and Klang rivers. This is the site of the original KL settlement in the 19th century, and has been occupied since 1909 by the graceful **Masjid Jamek ❷** (Jamek Mosque), the city's oldest mosque, with a sprawl of colonnades and spires around a peaceful square. Designed by colonial architect A.B. Hubback, it was the first mosque in KL to have an onion-shaped dome. Non-Muslims are not allowed to enter the mosque, so admire it from outside.

Oriental Building

Walk along the river towards the Masjid Jamek LRT station till you

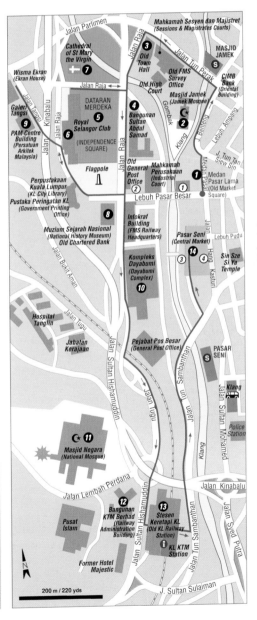

Food and Drink 🍴

① SIN SENG NAM RESTAURANT
2 Medan Pasar; no phone; Mon–Fri 7am–2.30pm; $
This old-style Hainanese coffee shop serves a favourite local breakfast. Start your day with toast and *kaya* (coconut and egg jam), a soft-boiled egg and thick coffee.

Old Theatre
The Old Town Hall hosts the lovely, old Panggung Bandaraya (City Hall Theatre), best known for having been gutted by fire in 1992 and under restoration for years. Check local listings for performances held here.

reach Jalan Tun Perak, which is perpendicular to Jalan Benteng. Across it, obscured by the LRT lines, is the **Oriental Building**, which houses the CIMB Bank. Like the clock tower on Medan Pasar Lama, this 1930s building was built in the Art Deco style, designed to look like an antique radio as a reflection of the identity of its original owner, Radio Malaya.

COLONIAL CORE

From the junction, turn left and walk past the LRT station along Jalan Tun Perak. This road leads to the city's colonial core, the most regal neighbourhood with Mughal-style public buildings. These were erected in the 1890s around the Dataran Merdeka (Independence Square) by the British administrators of the Federated Malay States (FMS). For some reason, the colonial architects of the Public Works Department deemed the Mughal style of architecture appropriate for the government buildings of the Malay peninsula. Featuring domes, minarets and arches, this distinct style was imported from another British outpost, India. After independence, most of these edifices served as courts before they were taken over in 2007 by the Ministry of Culture, Arts and Heritage as its offices.

Jalan Tun Perak
Walk along Jalan Tun Perak, skirting a long narrow building with a colonnade of clover-shaped arches on your left. This was once the **FMS Survey Office**, constructed in 1910, from

where public services were administered. The building hugs the corner of Jalan Tun Perak and Jalan Raja, and has its entrance facing Jalan Raja. Adjoining it is the **Old Town Hall ❸**, which, like the Survey Office, also sports a domed porch. Behind it, distinguished by pepper-pot turrets and double-columned arches, is the **Old High Court**. This trio of buildings used to house the Sessions and Magistrates Courts.

Jalan Raja
The boulevard in front of these buildings is **Jalan Raja**. It is off-limits to traffic on Saturday nights, when youngsters, couples and families hang out here or stroll along the road, enjoying the night breeze and bright lights that adorn the colonial buildings. Each June, this road explodes with the colours of a cultural parade that kicks off the Citrawarna Malaysia (Colours of Malaysia) tourism event.

Bangunan Sultan Abdul Samad
Walk across the bridge over the river and cross Jalan Raja at the pedestrian crossing to get to Dataran Merdeka. Once on the other side of the road, turn around for a good view of the magnificent **Bangunan Sultan Abdul Samad ❹** (Sultan Abdul Samad Building). The first Mughal-style building to be erected in the city, *c.*1897, it was once the colonial administrative centre, designed by colonial architects such as Arthur Charles Norman and R.A.J. Bidwell. Before it was built, KL had never had any-

thing like it, a work of symmetry with colonnades and notched parapets anchored by a square clock tower, stretching 137m (450ft) along Jalan Raja. Named after the Sultan of Selangor at the time, the building took three years to complete. A factory was even specially set up in the suburbs to supply the millions of bricks required to build it. Come back again at night to see this resplendent work; it is a very pretty sight when lit up.

INDEPENDENCE SQUARE

Turn to face **Dataran Merdeka ❺** (Independence Square). Once the British parade and cricket ground known as the Padang ('field' in Malay), this green was renamed after the country became a sovereign nation.

At the other side of the square is a cluster of Tudor-style buildings. This is another colonial relic, the members-only **Royal Selangor Club ❻**, built *c.*1884 and the nexus of British social life in the late 19th century. It still prides itself on an ambience that dates back to the days when Somerset Maugham was a regular visitor. The

club houses the Long Bar, which has existed since club membership was restricted to male colonials. Today, using the excuse of tradition, the gender bias remains: women are still not allowed into the Long Bar; nor are they allowed to vote in club elections or hold positions on the board.

ST MARY'S CATHEDRAL

To the right used to be the Royal Selangor Club's stables, which were flattened to make way for the church that stands there now, the **Cathedral of St Mary the Virgin ❼** (tel: 03-2692 8672; www.stmaryscathedral.org.my; daily 7am–3pm; free). Consecrated in 1887, St Mary's is one of the region's oldest Anglican churches and served as the main place of worship for the British in the colonial period. The current structure was rebuilt in the English Gothic style in 1922 following a fire. Its interesting architectural features include stained-glass windows with motifs of colonial planters and tropical crops such as rubber and oil palm, which were the agricultural mainstays of the peninsula's economy.

KELAB DI RAJA SELANGOR

Above from left:
Independence
Square; Victorian
fountain; erstwhile
home of Chow Kit
& Co.

Victorian Fountain

Walk towards the southern end of Dataran Merdeka. You will pass an ornate **Victorian fountain**. Some sources say it was brought from England to be placed at the Market Square, only to be moved to the field because the former site was too congested; others say it was built to honour a former British inspector of police.

Flagpole

The southern end of Dataran Merdeka is anchored by a **flagpole**, the tallest in

Malaysia and one of the tallest in the world. It was here at midnight on 31 August 1957 that England's Union Jack was lowered for the last time – on the shorter flagpole that used to stand here – and Malaysia became an independent nation. Since then, the field has been the venue for the annual countdown to National Day. At the stroke of midnight, the big clock at Bangunan Sultan Abdul Samad strikes to herald 31 August, accompanied by much revelry and fireworks. On 31 December every year, large crowds also gather here to count down to the New Year.

Across Jalan Raja, you can see a covered arched walkway linking the Bangunan Sultan Abdul Samad to the **Old General Post Office**, which has distinctive leaf-shaped pediments.

If you feel like a tea break, cross Jalan Raja and walk along the walkway through the passageway between the two buildings to get to **Colonial Cup**, see ①②, in the Straits Trading Building behind the Post Office. The Straits Trading Building houses the **Industrial Court**, which also occupies the historical building behind it, a corner pink-and-white edifice that was KL's first department store, Chow Kit & Co. This was established in the 1890s to cater to the colonials, offering everything from horse-riding gear to imported wines.

More Colonial Buildings

Otherwise, continue walking to the end of Dataran Merdeka, and straight ahead across Lebuh Pasar are two other historical buildings. At the

Malaysia Boleh

The giant flagpole in Dataran Merdeka is one of the many physical icons that were built at the tail end of the Mahathir era. After a decade of strong economic growth, Malaysia began to magnify itself in the eyes of the world as it worked towards achieving developed nation status by 2020. Best summed up with the catchphrase *Malaysia Boleh*

('Malaysia can do it'), record-setting in every aspect turned into a nation-building exercise. The results have ranged from the truly inspirational, like the achievements of the world number one squash player Nichol David, to the pitifully banal, like the making of the largest pizza in the shape of Malaysia. Cynics have used the phrase to describe embarrassing 'feats', particularly establishment-led endeavours that waste public funds.

corner is a three-storey Mughal-style structure, which was formerly the Muzium Sejarah Nasional (National History Museum) and originally served as the **Chartered Bank of India, Australia and China** ❽, where the colonial government held its accounts. Next to it is another period piece, the former **Government Printing Office**. A departure from the Mughal style, it has a no-frills neo-Renaissance design that reflects its functional purpose. Later, it served as the Perpustakaan Peringatan Kuala Lumpur (KL Memorial Library) until the new **Perpustakaan Kuala Lumpur** (KL City Library) was erected next to it. The new library has a large black dome, typifying the architect's attempt to incorporate Mughal features into a contemporary form.

PAM CENTRE

There are two options from the library. One is to head to Jalan Tangsi where another colonial gem dating back to 1907, the **PAM Centre Building** ❾, stands. To get there, walk past the Royal Selangor Club towards the Cathedral of St Mary the Virgin and cross the busy Jalan Kinabalu. The building, once the home of the millionaire Chow Kit, now hosts the **Persatuan Arkitek Malaysia** (Architects' Association of Malaysia; tel: 03-2693 4182; Mon–Fri 9am–5.30pm, Sat 9am–1pm; free). You can roam the halls of this neoclassical structure, which features Chinese artisanal craftsmanship and elegant details

such as Regency-style balconies. **Galeri Tangsi** (tel: 03-2691 0805; Mon–Fri 10.30am–6.30pm, Sat 10.30am–3pm; free), showcasing Malaysian and Asian art, is also here.

Ekran House

Walk to the end of Jalan Tangsi to look at another interesting piece of architecture. **Wisma Ekran** (Ekran House) is said to be one of the finest examples of Art Deco buildings in the city, complete with strong geometric forms and signature flagpoles.

Alternatively, from the library, head back to Jalan Raja and cross it, walking towards an orange-and-white building opposite the library. This was the colonial **FMS Railway Headquarters**, and later the Infokraf building, a striking building of ornamental rectangular columns and brick.

DAYABUMI COMPLEX

Jalan Raja becomes Jalan Sultan Hishamuddin further south. Walk south from Dataran Merdeka, take the left fork and you come to the gleaming white **Kompleks Dayabumi** ❿

Chow Kit & Co.
KL's first department store, Chow Kit & Co. *(shown above)*, was housed in this building. Early KL was built by rags-to-riches entrepreneurs such as Chow Kit, who scrimped and saved enough money to send back to their families in China. When they made their millions, they erected elaborate buildings to house their lucrative businesses and homes. These buildings have become legacies of the city.

Food and Drink 🍴
② **COLONIAL CUP**
G-08, Straits Trading Building, 2 Lebuh Pasar Baru; tel: 03-2697 5122; Mon–Fri 7.30am–4.30pm; $ This charming café with a skylight has a large breakfast selection until noon. Particularly good are the *roti jala* (lacy pancakes) and chicken curry, the 'colonial' fare such as bangers and mash, and egg-in-a-boat.

Dayabumi Complex
This tower marked the start of a trend of buildings with a local Islamic identity. The intricate fretwork also doubles as sun shades. This is also KL's first steel-frame skyscraper.

Below: the National Mosque has a dramatic roof design.

(Dayabumi Complex), a 35-storey structure completed in 1984 with fine filigree-like Islamic design. It is at its most impressive when it is floodlit at night. Go past the **General Post Office** (tel: 1300-300 300; Mon–Sat 8.30am–4.30 pm) and take the pedestrian underpass to the other side of Jalan Sultan Hishamuddin.

NATIONAL MOSQUE

Ahead is the **Masjid Negara** ⑪ (National Mosque; tel: 03-2693 7905; Mon–Thur 9am–noon, 3–4pm, 5.30–6.30pm, Fri for Muslim worshippers only), resplendent in white marble that is offset by pools of gurgling water. Following independence in 1957, buildings were designed in the Modernist style to reflect a progressive society. The Masjid Negara was completed in 1965; it is the first mosque to depart from the Mughal style and remains an icon of Modernism in Malaysian architecture today.

The mosque's circular, ridged blue roof symbolises an open umbrella, while its 73-m (240-ft) tall minaret represents a closed umbrella. There are various interpretations to the umbrella motif. It is said to echo the pyramidal roof form of traditional Malay houses and its 16 spokes represent the nation's 13 states (although it is unclear what the additional three spokes stand for). The mosque is also acknowledged as a symbol of national unity as it was built by, and with funds raised by, the country's various ethnic groups. It can accommodate up to 15,000 people.

If you wish to enter the mosque, remove your shoes, and use the robe provided if you are wearing shorts. Tour the interior to see the ornamental pools, fountains, a gallery and the Grand Prayer Hall. Non-Muslims, however, are forbidden to enter the prayer hall.

RAILWAY BUILDINGS

Down the road from the mosque, on the right, is the last of the Mughal-style buildings to be constructed, the **Bangunan KTM Berhad** ⑫ (Railway Administration Building), a stunning piece of architecture with a pastiche of various elements such as Mughal minarets, Gothic windows and Greek columns. It houses the offices of the Malaysian Railways.

The Bangunan KTM's features are echoed in another piece of colonial architectural extravagance designed by

A.B. Hubback, the **Stesen Keretapi Kuala Lumpur** ⓭ (Old KL Railway Station), which stands opposite. It can be accessed from the Bangunan KTM by an underpass. First completed in 1885, it was rebuilt at the turn of the century and extensively renovated in the 1980s. The bustle of human traffic has vanished since the interstate rail services were moved to the modern KL Sentral transport hub.

Go through the railway station to get to Jalan Tun Sambanthan. From Platform 1, head right until you reach an underpass and head for the exit on Platform 4. Occasionally, late at night, the famous and very expensive cream-and-green **Eastern and Oriental Express** (Singapore tel: 65-6392 3500; www.orient-express.com) train passes through on its way between Singapore in the south and Thailand up north. KTM Komuter trains head out from the centre platform to Port Klang, Seremban and Rawang.

CENTRAL MARKET

You now face Jalan Tun Sambanthan. Turn left and walk some 500m/yd to the **Central Market** ⓮ (Pasar Seni; tel: 03-2031 5399; www.central market-kl.com.my; daily 10am–10pm). Once the city's largest fresh-produce market, this was converted in the late 1980s into a cultural and shopping mall with conserved Art Deco features and a high ceiling. This is an excellent place to shop for souvenirs, including handicrafts, clothes, antiques and art, all at fairly reasonable prices.

Be sure to bargain, though. Along the side of the Central Market, Jalan Hang Kasturi is a pedestrian mall where other pre-war buildings have been turned into souvenir shops.

Market Annexe

The mall's **annexe** is a bustling arts space for performances and exhibitions; workshops and film screenings are also held here. On the ground floor, artists draw caricatures and portraits on the spot. A popular hang-out for Malay youth, guitarists among them, the Central Market is the birthplace and still the nexus of the local underground music scene, comprising rock bands whose faded jeans-clad members are known locally as Mat Rock.

For good Asian food, head to **Restaurant Ginger**, see ⑪③, or for simpler fare, **Restoran Yusoof dan Zakir**, see ⑪④, just outside the mall.

Food and Drink 🍴

③ RESTAURANT GINGER

Lot M12, Central Market; tel: 03-2273 7371; daily 11am–10pm; $$
Order the spicy Malay *rendang* (dry beef or chicken curry), Thai green chicken curry and Indonesian fried rice accompanied by *satay* at this sumptuously decorated restaurant.

④ RESTORAN YUSOOF DAN ZAKIR

44 & 46 Jalan Hang Kasturi; tel: 03-2026 8685; daily 24 hours; $
An eatery abuzz with locals who come for the good variety of Indian *roti* (breads). Service is quick – your *roti* arrives within minutes of ordering.

PETALING STREET

A tourist magnet and a bargain hunter's paradise most famous for its street bazaar, Petaling Street also offers plenty of eateries, temples and clanhouses, many of which have survived from the time of the city's beginnings.

Facelift
In 2003, Petaling Street was given a facelift to make it more 'distinctly Chinese'. A stock gateway typically found in Chinatowns all over the world, where Chinese are newer migrants, was added. This was despite the fact that the Chinese are KL's majority ethnic group, making up 40 percent of the population.

DISTANCE 4½km (2¾ miles)
TIME A full day
START Petaling Street Gateway
END Sin Sze Si Ya Temple
POINTS TO NOTE
From the Pasar Seni LRT station, turn right onto Jalan Tun Tan Cheng Lock and walk about 500m/yd to the junction of Jalan Petaling and Jalan Tun Tan Cheng Lock.

The city's most famous street bazaar is often just referred to by the name of the main road it occupies: Petaling Street (Jalan Petaling). It sits in a bustling part of KL, dominated by pre-war Chinese-style shophouses. Although largely Chinese in character, the area also bears influences from other ethnic groups.

PETALING STREET MARKET

Bargain Hard
Prices at the Petaling Street Bazaar are grossly inflated, so bargain hard and shop around, as you can usually find the same products at other stalls.

From the **Petaling Street Gateway**, walk down Jalan Petaling, turn right onto Jalan Hang Lekir and look out for an entrance next to Hotel Malaya. This leads to the **Petaling Street Market ❶** (daily 7am–3pm). Go early to experience the action and smells in this small, century-old fresh-produce market with vegetables, seafood, poultry and more.

PETALING STREET BAZAAR

Head back onto Jalan Petaling. On the left corner is a famous stall selling the *mata kucing* herbal drink, see ①. The **Petaling Street Bazaar ❷** comes alive at around 10am along Jalan Petaling and Jalan Hang Lekir. During the day, the stalls occupy the pavements in front of the shops, spilling onto the road. From 4.30 to 11pm, Jalan Petaling is closed to traffic and vendors take over the road to form the noisiest and most exciting night market in KL. The stalls offer mainly knock-offs of branded goods; there are also souvenirs, fruits and snacks.

Food and Drink

① MATA KUCING DRINK STALL
Corner of Jalan Hang Lekir and Jalan Petaling; daily 10am–10pm; $
Serving the cooling local drink *mata kucing* (literally 'cat's eye'), made with three Asian fruits, including *longan*.

② CHINATOWN SENG KEE
50 Jalan Sultan; tel: 03-2072 5950; daily 11am–4.30pm; $
Try its excellent Chinese-style noodles like the KL speciality Hokkien *mee* (noodles stir-fried in dark soy sauce) and claypot *loh shu fun* (rice noodles in a minced-pork sauce).

Petaling Street and its surroundings make for a wonderful browse in the daytime. From the second Chinese gateway at the southern end of Jalan Petaling, you have two options. Turn left to explore Jalan Sultan, with Chinese tea shops, traditional businesses and old-style eateries like **Chinatown Seng Kee**, see ①②. Otherwise, if you continue south, you come to shops piled with things plastic and shiny – this is the city's wholesale hub of knick-knacks and fashion accessories. Buried here are a few old-style businesses, such as the coffin shop at no. 135 and the incense retailer at no. 124.

CHAN SHE SHU YUEN

At the corner of Jalan Petaling and Jalan Stadium sits the **Chan She Shu Yuen Association ③** (tel: 03-2078 1461; daily 8am–5pm; free). This clan association has been looking after the needs of Chinese people with the surnames Chan, Chen and Tan since 1896. Note its roof, decorated with intricate ceramic figurines and wall friezes depicting Chinese mythology and history.

GUAN YIN TEMPLE

Across Jalan Stadium from the Chan She Shu Yuen Association is the delightful **Guan Yin Temple ④** (tel: 03-2070 8650; daily 8am–5pm; free), located at the top of a flight of steps guarded by a pair of stone lions. This century-old Hokkien temple has an image of a thousand-armed and thousand-eyed Guan Yin, the Goddess of

Mercy. This is one of the few Hokkien temples in town, with a curved roof typical of such temples.

CHINESE ASSEMBLY HALL

Clan associations are community groups formed in the 19th century by Chinese immigrants. These associations later became the Associated Chinese Chambers of Commerce. The national headquarters of the chambers was once located opposite the Chan She Shu Yuen Association. This is now the **Chinese Assembly Hall ⑤**, housed in a white colonial-era building capped by a dome. Cross the overhead

Above: ceramic figures on the roof of Chan She Shu Yuen; Goddess of Mercy at the Guan Yin Temple; entrance of the clan association.

Clanhouses
The two largest groups of 19th-century Chinese migrants to Malaysia are the Cantonese and the Hokkien. Both were served by Chinese clanhouses, which comprised not just temples, but also provided accommodation, education, financial help and more.

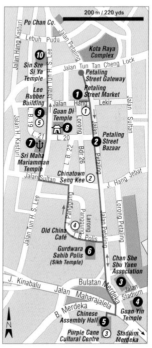

Tea Shop
Purple Cane also
has a little shop
selling Chinese tea
products. You can
ask for an explanation
of the different types
of Chinese tea and
see a tea-brewing
demonstration
(below opposite).

pedestrian bridge over Jalan Maharajalela to get to the hall. The building hosts exhibitions and talks. The left corner of the building is taken up by the **Purple Cane Cultural Centre**, an excellent choice for lunch; see ⑪③.

JALAN BALAI POLIS

After lunch, return to Jalan Petaling and turn left onto Jalan Balai Polis. On your left is the **Gurdwara Sahib Polis** ❻ (daily 9am–5pm; free). Sikhs were originally brought from India to the Malay states by the British to staff the police force and once made up its majority. A simple structure wearing

the blue of Malaysian police buildings, it houses the *Guru Granth Sahib*, the Sikh holy book.

Opposite the Sikh temple is the **Old China Café**, see ⑪④, serving Nonya (Peranakan) food and a potential spot for dinner. Behind its swinging doors, black-and-white photos and heavy marble-topped tables add to its delightful old-world atmosphere.

From Jalan Balai Polis, turn right onto Jalan Panggung, then left onto Jalan Sultan and right again onto Jalan Tun H.S. Lee. Named after a politician who was instrumental in helping Malaya gain independence from the British, Jalan Tun H.S. Lee is lined

Stadium Merdeka

Steps from the side entrance of the Guan Yin Temple lead to the Maharajalela Monorail Station and a car park, beyond which stands the Stadium Merdeka. Built in time for Malaya's independence on 31 August 1957, the stadium is witness to the most iconic moment in the country's modern history: that of the first prime minister Tunku Abdul Rahman punching his fist in the air and shouting 'Merdeka' ('independence') seven times. It later fell into disrepair and would have been demolished if not for the 1997 Asian financial crisis, which bankrupted its developers. It is now being restored under the management of the Heritage of Malaysia Trust.

Food and Drink 🍴

③ PURPLE CANE
1 Jalan Maharajalela; tel: 03-2272
3090; www.purplecane.com.my;
daily 11.30am–7pm; $
This serves 'tea cuisine' prepared
with premium Chinese tea leaves.
Try the simmered black-tea chicken
with tea rice and the mushroom
chicken cooked in *pu'er* tea.

④ OLD CHINA CAFÉ
11 Jalan Balai Polis; tel: 03-2072
5915; daily 11am–10.30pm; $$
The charming setting is perfect for
Nonya specialities such as *ayam
pongteh* (chicken stew) and *asam
prawns* (tamarind prawns).

⑤ PETER HOE BEYOND
2/F, Lee Rubber Building, 145 Jalan
Tun H.S. Lee; tel: 03-2026 9788;
daily 10am–7pm; $
Order tasty treats including quiches,
pastas and burgers. The tofu and
orange salad and baked pumpkin
soup are recommended.

with elaborate 19th-century shop-houses. It used to be called High Street because it was higher than the surrounding streets and therefore not as prone to flooding.

SRI MAHA MARIAMMAN TEMPLE

About 50m/yd along Jalan Tun H.S. Lee is a gateway tower adorned with statues of Hindu deities. This is the entrance to the **Sri Maha Mariamman Temple** ❼ (tel: 03-2078 3467; daily 6am–1am; free). Dedicated to the Mother Goddess Mariamman, the temple is laid out in the shape of the human body. The gateway represents the feet, marking the threshold between the material and the spiritual worlds. Built in 1873, the temple occupies an important place in Hindu religious life; the annual Thaipusam procession to Batu Caves *(see p.64)* begins from here.

GUAN DI TEMPLE

Diagonally opposite the Hindu temple is one of the finest Cantonese temples in the city, the **Guan Di Temple** ❽ (daily 7am–5pm; free). It honours the red-faced Guan Di, the God of War and Literature, and the Tiger God, who is worshipped during the Lunar New Year to ward off troublemakers. Built in 1888, the temple is also known as the Kwong Siew Temple because it was built by the Kwong Siew Association, which represents many of KL's original Cantonese families.

LEE RUBBER BUILDING

The **Lee Rubber Building** ❾ is further along Jalan Tun H.S. Lee. Its narrow Art Deco-style facade features vertical bands that emphasise the building's height. Built by one of the country's most successful rubber companies, it houses an excellent souvenir shop, **Peter Hoe Beyond**, and a charming **café**, see ⑪⑤.

SIN SZE SI YA TEMPLE

Continue along Jalan Tun H.S. Lee, cross Jalan Tun Tan Cheng Lock and enter a discreet doorway adorned with dragons on the left to the Taoist **Sin Sze Si Ya Temple** ❿ (tel: 03-2072 9593; daily 7am–5pm; free).

Constructed according to feng shui principles, the temple entrance oddly faces a corner. It was built by the Chinese leader Yap Ah Loy in 1864 to honour two of his comrades, Sin Sze Ya and Si Sze Ya. Their altars are in the main hall. After his death in 1885, Yap was also enshrined in the temple.

Above from far left: a faithful lights incense at the Sin Sze Si Ya Temple; petitions at the temple.

Hindu Worship
Like most Hindu temples, the Sri Maha Mariamman Temple is busiest in the early morning and evening. This is when the curtain concealing the statue of the main deity is unveiled and bathed by the priest who also conducts prayers. Remove your shoes before entering.

Left: tea-brewing demonstration at Purple Cane.

3

KUALA LUMPUR CITY CENTRE

This tour around KL's business district focuses on the Petronas Twin Towers and Menara Kuala Lumpur, both of which afford fabulous views. Their surroundings entice with great nature, shopping and nightlife.

Fireworks
The Petronas Twin Towers serve as the backdrop for spectacular fireworks on New Year's Eve and National Day (31 August). Check with Tourism Malaysia (hotline: 1300-885 050; www.tourism. gov.my) for details.

DISTANCE 2km (1¼ miles)
TIME A full day
START Petronas Twin Towers
END Menara Kuala Lumpur
POINTS TO NOTE

Take the LRT to the underground KLCC LRT station, which is linked to the Suria KLCC mall at the base of the Petronas Twin Towers. Aim to end the tour in the evening; the area offers numerous nightlife options.

The 40-ha (100-acre) **Kuala Lumpur City Centre** (KLCC), one of the largest real estate developments in the world, is situated on the site of the former Selangor Turf Club. The focal point of a country charging towards developed-nation status, KLCC comprises offices, which are housed in the gleaming Petronas Twin Towers and the surrounding skyscrapers, the Suria KLCC shopping mall, a beautiful landscaped park, convention centre, aquarium and several luxury hotels.

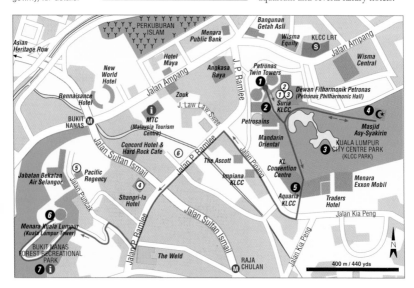

PETRONAS TWIN TOWERS

The **Petronas Twin Towers** ❶, soaring 452m (1,483ft) into the sky, are the anchor of KLCC. These towers were once the world's tallest buildings, a record held from April 1996 to October 2003. Now, as proud Malaysians are keen to point out, the towers remain the world's tallest *pair* of buildings.

Named after and owned by the national petroleum and gas company, the towers were designed by the renowned US-based architect Cesar Pelli and were built at the hefty price tag of US$1.2 billion, using 65,000sq m (700,000sq ft) of stainless-steel cladding, 160,000 cubic m (5.7 million cubic ft) of concrete and 77,000sq m (830,000sq ft) of glass. The design of the towers reflects a concerted effort to express a Malaysian identity. For instance, the floor plans of the towers take after an eight-point star formed from two interlocking squares, a popular Islamic architectural motif, while the number of storeys – 88 – translates as 'double luck' in Chinese.

Good views of the Twin Towers can be had from the adjoining KLCC Park, though photography angles are better from Jalan Ampang and Jalan Tun Razak, as well as from the upper floors of various hotels in the area.

Skybridge

A 58.4-m (192-ft) double-deck **skybridge** (tel: 03-2331 7619; Tue–Sun 9am–7pm; free) links the two towers on levels 41 and 42. Although the view from here is not as spectacular as that from the Menara Kuala Lumpur *(see p.41)* or from the surrounding hotels, a trip to the skybridge is still a must for many tourists. Groups of 20 are allowed entry at 15-minute intervals. You can queue up for tickets from 8am onwards at the concourse level of Tower Two; a maximum of 1,600 tickets are issued per day.

SURIA KLCC

At the base of the towers sits **Suria KLCC** ❷ (tel: 03-2382 3359; daily 10am–10pm), a spacious, classy shopping mall with department stores and over 270 speciality shops. Of particular note is **Aseana** (Lot G13-19; tel: 03-2382 9988), a gallery of boutiques on the ground floor that is wonderful for browsing; it features a range of Southeast Asian handicraft, batik and

Above from far left: on the skybridge of the Petronas Twin Towers; glittering towers; indoor café in Suria KLCC.

Above: international boutiques at Suria KLCC.

Below: Aseana.

collectibles. The **Pucuk Rebung Royal Gallery-Museum** (Lot 302-A; tel: 03-2382 1109) is a private museum with beautiful collections of Malaysian artefacts, antiques and objets d'art, some of which are for sale.

Science Museum and Art Gallery

Children can easily spend hours at **Petrosains** (tel: 03-2331 8787; Tue–Sun 9.30am–5.30pm; charge), on Level 6 of Suria KLCC. This is an excellent interactive museum on the oil and gas industry for families, run by Petronas. The national petroluem company also owns the elegant art gallery **Galeri Petronas** (Petronas Gallery; tel: 03-2331 7770; www.galeri petronas.com; Tue–Sun 10am–8pm; free) on Level 3. Contemporary and traditional works are exhibited here.

There are numerous eateries and food courts in Suria KLCC. Recommended are **Chinoz on the Park**, see Ⓨ①, **Aseana Café**, see Ⓨ②, and **Signatures Food Court**, see Ⓨ③.

KLCC PARK

Once the day cools down a little, head out to the **Suria Esplanade** to explore the **KLCC Park ❸**. The 'dancing' fountains on the lake fronting the Esplanade are a favourite with locals. Beyond the lake is a 20-ha (50-acre) artfully laid-out garden designed by the late Brazilian landscape artist Roberto Burle Marx. A jogging track winds around the lake, past fountains, sculptures and vegetation. The trees and shrubs in the park comprise mainly indigenous species. About 40 trees were kept intact during the construction of KLCC and date back to the time when the area was the Selangor Turf Club. Children will enjoy the playground and wading pool (Tue–Sun 10am–7.30pm; free).

Asy-Syakirin Mosque

In the grounds also is the **Masjid Asy-Syakirin ❹** (Asy-Syakirin Mosque; tel: 03-2380 1291; daily 9am–5pm, except prayer times), featuring a metallic dome and delicate Islamic calligraphy. The dome has diamond-shaped apertures that allow sunlight to enter the mosque during the day and the inside light to radiate out at night.

Convention Centre and Aquarium

Now return to the Suria Esplanade and skirt around Suria KLCC to get

Below: bird's-eye view of KLCC Park.

to the **Kuala Lumpur Convention Centre**, a high-tech space for trade shows and conventions, where concerts and theatre performances are sometimes staged. Its concourse level is occupied by the **Aquaria KLCC** ❺ (tel: 03-2333 1888; www.klaquaria.com; daily 11am–8pm, last entry at 7pm; charge), a family-friendly interactive rainforest exhibition space and aquarium with more than 5,000 fish and other marine creatures. The submerged tunnel with a moving walkway is a particular highlight.

KUALA LUMPUR TOWER

The best place to get a 360-degree, bird's-eye view of the city is from the **Menara Kuala Lumpur** ❻ (Kuala Lumpur Tower; tel: 03-2020 5444; www.menarakl.com.my; daily 9am–10pm; charge). To get there from Aquaria KLCC, exit onto Jalan Pinang and turn right. Walk along the road and turn left onto Jalan P. Ramlee. One of downtown KL's nightlife hubs, the road is named after a late Malaysian entertainment icon. His songs and

Above from far left: kids have fun with the interactive exhibits at Petrosains; 'dancing' fountains at KLCC Park; Aquaria KLCC.

Food and Drink 🍴

① CHINOZ ON THE PARK
Lot G47, G/F, Suria KLCC; tel: 03-2166 8277; daily 10am–10pm; $$
Great alfresco dining overlooking the KLCC Park. The menu leans towards Mediterranean food but there are pastas, pizzas and sandwiches (try the salted beef on rye and apple sauerkraut sandwich).

② ASEANA CAFÉ
Lot G11–20, G/F, Suria KLCC; tel: 03-2382 0395; daily 10am–10pm; $
Located inside Aseana, this has snacks such as the decadent *goreng pisang a la bali* (banana fritters) and *ubi rebus* (steamed tapioca) served with grated coconut or spicy sambal *ikan bilis*.

③ SIGNATURES FOOD COURT
2/F, Suria KLCC; tel: 03-2382 2828; daily 10am–10pm; $–$$
This popular 28-outlet food court offers a good variety, from pasta to tandoori dishes and ice-cream to Thai desserts. Local and regional favourites include Ipoh noodles, Thai green curry and Taiwanese beef noodles.

Millionaires' Row

The road in front of the Petronas Twin Towers' main entrance is Jalan Ampang, where Kuala Lumpur millionaires of the late 19th and early 20th century built their mansions. Many of these buildings feature an eclectic combination of Oriental and Occidental architectural elements, such as Chinese moongates that flank Roman pillars. A number of them have fallen prey to changing values and weak conservation laws. One victim was the neoclassical Bok House, one of Jalan Ampang's most magnificent specimens built by a pioneer to woo his lady love. It was demolished in 2006. Thankfully, other mansions remain. At no. 109 is a graceful 1935 château that now houses the Malaysia Tourism Centre (tel: 03-9235 4848; www.mtc.gov.my; daily 8am–10pm). Opposite it at no. 132 is an elegant bungalow that, like the MTC, sports an octagonal tower; it is now the Pakistan High Commission. Postmodern architecture has also crept into Jalan Ampang. Structures include no. 113, the pod-shaped Zouk, one of the city's hottest nightspots. Facing it is the slick Hotel Maya with its imaginative use of space and materials.

Tower Aids
The Menara Kuala Lumpur has a self-guiding audio tour in several languages and binoculars, which provide good views of the city.

Which is Taller?
Although the Menara Kuala Lumpur is shorter than the Petronas Twin Towers, the former actually surpasses the latter in terms of height above sea level because it sits on top of a hill.

Below: view from the Menara KL.

movies, produced mainly in the 1950s and 1960s, are well-loved classics that continue to influence contemporary entertainers. Walk past the clubs and pubs and cross the Jalan Sultan Ismail junction. The Shangri-La hotel is on your right. Its **Cinnamon** café, see ⑪④, serves delicious pastries. If you don't stop for tea, continue up the slope and turn onto Jalan Puncak on your right. Another left turn takes you to the Menara Kuala Lumpur.

Tower Architecture
A super-swift lift delivers you up to the **observation deck** of the 421-m (138-ft) tall Menara Kuala Lumpur. If weather permits, this is probably the best place to admire views of the Petronas Twin Towers and the city. The tower head is inspired by the Malaysian *gasing*, a top that is used in a traditional game, and the tower's design reflect an influence of Islamic motifs. Of note are the arches of the

entrance lobby, which are adorned with glass that resemble diamonds. The building also has souvenir shops, cafés and a revolving restaurant. Cultural shows (Thur–Sun 4–4.45pm; free) are held at the amphitheatre.

Extreme Sports
The Menara Kuala Lumpur has also become an extreme sports venue. Try the 'flying fox' (daily 11am–7pm, unavailable on rainy days; charge), where you are winched down on an inclined 100-m (330-ft) long rope from the lower balcony of the tower. Two established and popular annual

---

Food and Drink

④ CINNAMON
Lobby Floor, Shangri-La Hotel; tel: 03-2032 2388 ext. 1341; daily 7am–10pm; $$
This cinnamon-themed coffee bar is popular for its freshly baked pastries. It offers an assortment of cinnamon flavoured muffins, sticky buns and pretzels, and serves good coffee.

⑤ LUNA BAR
34/F, Pacific Regency Hotel Suites, Jalan Puncak; tel: 03-2332 7777; daily 5pm–3am; $$$
This outdoor, rooftop bar boasts a pool in the middle and amazing view. Remember to bring your camera.

⑥ POPPY COLLECTION
18-1 Jalan P. Ramlee; tel: 03-2141 8888; daily meals 8am–10pm, bar 10pm–2am (3am on weekends); $$
Start with pre-dinner cocktails, move on to a Thai main course and end with wine in this stylish glass-and-garden setting. Upstairs is the techno club, Passion.

events are held here: the Kuala Lumpur International Forest Towerthon, a race up Bukit Nanas and the tower, and the Kuala Lumpur Tower International Jump, which involves BASE jumping (parachute-aided free-falling). Check the Menara Kuala Lumpur website for activity dates.

BUKIT NANAS FOREST RECREATIONAL PARK

The Menara Kuala Lumpur sits in the **Bukit Nanas Forest Recreational Park** ❼ (daily 7am–6pm; free), the country's oldest forest reserve, gazetted in 1906. Bukit Nanas is the only remaining green lung in the brick-and-mortar clutter of the Golden Triangle. If there is still light after you have visited the Menara Kuala Lumpur, you might want to explore the forest park. It has five short and well-marked trails that wind through the shady rainforest, which is rich with insects, monkeys, birds and primary forest plant species.

Be sure to wear insect repellent before you enter the forest and do check in first at the **Forest Information Centre** on Jalan Raja Chulan. You can also go on one of the free 45-minute tours (11am, 12.30pm, 2.30pm and 4.30pm) conducted by the Menara Kuala Lumpur; wait at the ground floor of the tower.

ENTERTAINMENT HUB

There are several nightlife options in the KLCC area. The most accessible option from the Menara Kuala Lumpur is **Luna Bar**, see ⓰⑤. To get there, walk down the hill and cross Jalan Puncak to the Pacific Regency Hotel Suites where it is located.

Another option is to return to Suria KLCC, where you can dine at one of its many eateries. After dinner, chill out at the Suria Esplanade or opt for a music performance at the **Dewan Filharmonik Petronas** (box office tel: 03-2051 7007; www.malaysianphil harmonic.com; dress code applies). Located at the podium level of the Petronas Twin Towers, this is the home of the Malaysian Philharmonic Orchestra. Fashioned after a 19th-century European concert hall, this venue, though small, has excellent acoustics.

Party-goers may want to check out the entertainment hub of **Jalan P. Ramlee**, **Jalan Sultan Ismail** and **Jalan Pinang**. The club scene here throbs with action until the early hours of the morning. **Poppy Collection**, see ⓰⑥, on Jalan P. Ramlee, is a long-standing favourite. **Asian Heritage Row**, on Jalan Doraisamy off Jalan Sultan Ismail, is an enclave of trendy bars and restaurants contained within restored pre-war houses.

Above from far left: glass-studded Islamic-inspired arch at the KL Tower; Silver Leaf monkey resident of the Bukit Nanas Forest Park; Bukit Nanas has well-marked trails; nightlife action on Jalan P. Ramlee.

Cheap Tickets Tickets for the Malaysian Philharmonic Orchestra's matinee concerts can go for as little as RM10. The orchestra also has interesting concerts for children as part of its 'Family Fun Days' programme.

Below: Asian Heritage Row.

THE LAKE GARDENS AND BANGSAR

A haven of landscaped greenery in the city, the Lake Gardens' numerous parks and museums can easily occupy a full day. Nearby is the upmarket Bangsar area, great for international cafés, restaurants and shopping.

DISTANCE 5km (3 miles)

TIME A full day

START Tugu Kebangsaan

END Bangsar Baru

POINTS TO NOTE

Rapid Bus no. B115 from the Kota Raya shopping centre near Petaling Street stops on Jalan Parlimen; from here walk and turn right to get to Tugu Kebangsaan and left to the Lake Gardens. The Kuala Lumpur Hop-on Hop-off bus *(see p.106)* also stops at the entrance of the Lake Gardens; cross the road to get to the monument. Start the day early and enjoy the gardens in cooler weather.

Parliament House

From the ASEAN Sculpture Garden, turn right and walk along Jalan Parlimen for a good look at the Parliament House. Built after independence, it has a tower block clad with sunshades, which resembles the skin of a pineapple, and a podium of triangular structures inspired by the traditional Malay roof form.

Alfred Venning, the former British State Treasurer, was more interested in creating a paradisiacal botanical garden amid lakes in the heart of KL than in making money. Now, over 120 years later, the name Venning scarcely means anything to KL-ites, but his legacy lives on in the heart of the city.

THE LAKE GARDENS

The **Lake Gardens** (Taman Tasik Perdana; daily 24 hours; free), with 104ha (257 acres) of close-cropped lawns, undulating hills and cultivated gardens, is a sanctuary from the maddening mayhem of the city. The leafy gardens is also a valuable green lung, helping to cleanse the city of its polluted air.

The Lake Gardens are popular with exercise enthusiasts, from joggers to t'ai chi practitioners, at dawn and dusk. Families throng the area on weekends, with picnic baskets in hand. On Sunday mornings, a free communal aerobics session is held in the Panggung Aniversari Amphitheatre.

In the gardens are other attractions, including a deer park with several local species; a bird park, with one of the region's largest aviaries; a butterfly park, a sanctuary for over 6,000 butterflies and moths; and an orchid garden and hibiscus garden, with hundreds of luxuriant blooms.

You will not have time to visit all the attractions, so plan ahead. If you want to avoid walking in the hot and humid weather, opt for the park shuttle bus (daily 10am–5.30pm, except 1–2pm), which leaves from the boathouse near the lake. It makes stops at the main attractions. The Kuala Lumpur Hop-on Hop-off service *(see p.106)* also goes through the gardens.

National Monument

The **Tugu Kebangsaan ❶** (National Monument) commemorates local and foreign servicemen who died during the Communist insurgency of 1948–60. It was modelled after the Iwo Jima memorial in the US. Steps lead down to a **cenotaph** commemorating the soldiers who died in the two World Wars.

ASEAN Sculpture Garden

Walk down the hill and through the **ASEAN Sculpture Garden ❷** (free). The sculptures are symbols of the alliance among the 10 nations of the Association of Southeast Asian Nations, of which Malaysia is a member.

BUTTERFLY PARK

From the junction of Jalan Parlimen and Jalan Cenderawasih, walk on for 300m/yd and turn left to the **Butterfly Park ❸** (tel: 03-2693 4799; daily 9am–6pm; charge), on Jalan Cenderasari. This pretty garden has thousands of plants that help re-create the insects' natural habitats. One of its buildings houses a collection of Malaysia's rainforest insects, reptiles and amphibians. **Nasi Lemak Tanglin**, see ⑪①, further down the road, serves a favourite Malaysian breakfast.

Food and Drink 🍴

① NASI LEMAK TANGLIN

Jalan Cenderasari; Mon–Fri 7am–noon and 4.30–9.30pm, Sat–Sun 7am–noon; $
A famous outlet serving *nasi lemak* – fragrant coconut rice with *ikan bilis sambal* (anchovies cooked with chilli), peanuts and cucumber.

Above from far left: ASEAN Sculpture Garden; the National Monument pays tribute to soldiers who fought against Communists; Butterfly Park.

T'ai Chi
Anyone is welcome to join in a t'ai chi session at the Lake Gardens. These are usually led by volunteers and participants are usually retirees. Sessions are held very early, often before 7am.

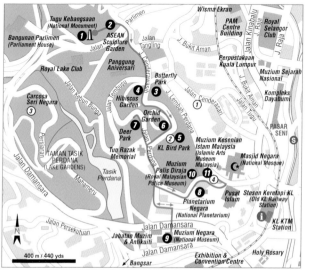

HIBISCUS GARDEN

At this point, head back to Jalan Cenderawasih. Located diagonally across from the junction is the entrance to the **Hibiscus Garden** ❹ (daily 9am–6pm; weekdays free, weekend charge). It is a riot of colours with 2,500 hibiscus plants of different varieties from all over the world. Malaysian forests are home to several species of hibiscus, but, for some reason, the species that was chosen as Malaysia's national flower *(bunga raya)* is actually not native to the country but originates from Hawaii.

BIRD PARK

Continue on Jalan Cenderawasih to the **Kuala Lumpur Bird Park** ❺ (tel: 03-2272 1010; daily 9am–6pm; charge). This 8-ha (20-acre) covered aviary is home to 3,000 birds of over 200 species. Except for a few free-flying species, most are housed in display and confined areas. Of note is the hornbill section, where you get close-up views of these large black-and-white creatures with prominent beaks and magnificent tails. Malaysia has 10 species of hornbills, some of which figure in the rites and beliefs of certain indigenous people. An excellent place to view them is the **Hornbill Restoran & Kafe**, see ⑪②, located within the hornbill section.

ORCHID GARDEN

Opposite the Bird Park is the **Orchid Garden** ❻ (daily 9am–6pm; weekdays free, weekend charge). There are about 2,000 orchid species in Malaysia. About 800-odd species are grown in the Orchid Garden, a mix of both cultivated and wild orchids, and many specimens are on sale.

DEER PARK

From the Orchid Garden, turn right onto Jalan Cenderawasih and walk on until you reach the T-junction. Turn right onto Jalan Perdana to the **Deer Park** ❼ (Mon–Thur 10am–noon and 2–6pm, Fri 10am–noon and 3–6pm, Sat–Sun 10am–6pm; free), which will

Lake Gardens
There are more species of flora in Malaysia alone than in the entire North American continent. The Lake Gardens are not only an oasis in the heart of KL but also an excellent place to view a riotous display of colours.

Orchid Souvenirs
Orchids packed in flasks that are travel-safe make great souvenirs from the Orchid Garden. These also come with instructions on their cultivation.

Food and Drink 🍽

② HORNBILL RESTORAN & KAFE
Kuala Lumpur Bird Park, Jalan Cenderawasih; tel: 03-2693 8086; daily 9am–7pm; $
The fan-cooled verandah is a good spot to view the hornbills. Try the fried *mee mamak*, spicy noodles with seafood and potatoes or the fish and chips.

③ CARCOSA SERI NEGARA
Lake Gardens; tel: 03-2295 0888; daily noon–3pm and 7–10.30pm; www.ghmhotels.com; $$$
The Gulai House serves fine Malay and North Indian cuisines. Its Sunday curry tiffin lunch is a must-try. The Dining Room serves exquisite award-winning French food. There is a dress code for indoor dining but not for the pleasant garden-facing verandah. English tea with scones and cucumber sandwiches are also served in The Drawing Room (daily 3–6pm).

appeal to children. The highlight here is the shy mousedeer, the smallest deer in the world; it's about the size of a cat. The park has been successfully breeding these animals. Visitors can also feed Mauritian and Dutch deer.

CARCOSA SERI NEGARA

By now it is lunchtime. If the simple Hornbill Restoran & Kafé at the Bird Park does not appeal, consider the **Carcosa Seri Negara** hotel, see ⑪③. Note that it is a bit of a trek across the gardens, but the hotel is an attraction on its own. The mock-Tudor Carcosa, built in 1896, was once the residence of British officials. It is now a luxury hotel, along with another mansion, the Seri Negara, which sits on an adjoining hill.

NATIONAL PLANETARIUM

After lunch, continue on Jalan Perdana past the **Tun Razak Memorial**, which honours Malaysia's second prime minister. After about 500m/yd, you reach the **Planetarium Negara** ❽ (National Planetarium; tel: 03-2273 5484; Tue–Sun 9.30am–4.30pm; charge). It has a 36-cm (14-inch) telescope and also houses the Arianne IV space engine that launched Malaysia's first satellite, the Measat I. Its well-designed garden is dotted with replicas of ancient observatories.

NATIONAL MUSEUM

A pedestrian bridge behind the planetarium leads to the **Muzium Negara** ❾

(National Museum; tel: 03-2282 6255; www.museum.gov.my; daily 9am–6pm; charge). The museum's exhibits are uninspiring but its architecture is outstanding. This is the first post-independence building designed in the neotraditional instead of the Modernist style, reflecting the national identity of a new sovereign country. Its roofs are inspired by traditional Malay roofs and, perched on 26 pillars, the building is laid out like a Malay palace. Two massive batik murals depict the highlights of Malaysian history and culture.

POLICE MUSEUM

If you are keen to visit more museums, head back to the planetarium and onto Jalan Perdana to get to the **Muzium Polis Diraja Malaysia** ❿ (Royal

Above from far left: feeding time at the Bird Park; batik mural at the National Museum traces Malaysian history and culture; the Carcosa Seri Negara; long flight of steps leading to the blue-domed National Planetarium.

Below: an old steam train at the National Museum.

White Dome

A beautiful white inverted dome *(see below)* with gold inscriptions of the opening verse of the Quran adorn the ground floor of the Islamic Arts Museum. It is one of the museum's five domes, which represent the five pillars of Islam.

Below: the White Dome at the Islamic Arts Museum.

Malaysian Police Museum; tel: 03-2272 5689; Tue–Sun 10am–6pm, Fri closed 12.30–2.30pm; free). Children can explore armoured tanks and the police force's first aircraft – a single-engined Cessna. The Weapons section is among the most popular, featuring guns from post-World War II China-aligned Communist guerillas.

ISLAMIC ARTS MUSEUM

From the Police Museum, continue on Jalan Perdana and turn right onto Jalan Lembah Perdana to the **Muzium Kesenian Islam Malaysia ⓫** (Islamic Arts Museum Malaysia; tel: 03-2274 2020; www.iamm.org.my; daily 10am–6pm; charge). This spacious private museum is a dignified repository of

artefacts from the Islamic world, with temporary exhibitions on the lower floors and permanent collections on the two upper floors.

Of note are the intricate architectural models of famous monuments and structures of the Islamic era, such as the Indian Taj Mahal and famous mosques of the holy city of Medinah. Another highlight is the Ottoman Room, which is dedicated to the period considered as the Renaissance of Islamic Arts (1453–1923). Other displays include manuscripts, ceramics, textiles, jewellery and metalwork.

There are also facilities for kids, such as a children's library with games and weekend book-reading activities, as well as a souvenir shop selling textiles, artwork, books, crystals and replicas of Islamic artefacts. Have a coffee and snack or a full meal at the **Museum Restaurant**, see ⑪④.

BANGSAR

After a tour of the museums, take a taxi to **Bangsar**, the first definitive area for the city's affluent and trendy. It is one of the most exclusive residential addresses in KL, with a density of bungalows and luxury condominiums popular with expatriates. Bangsar used to be just a watering hole, with chic bars, clubs and eateries great for people-watching, but it has metamorphosed into a shopping and family-oriented hub, particularly with the addition of higher-end malls. Nonetheless, Bangsar still has modish bars, coffee houses and beautiful people who come out at night. Among the

more popular are pubs like **Canteena's**, **Ronnie Q's** and **Finnegan's**, as well as the trendsetting **Alexis Bistro**, see ⑪⑤, and **La Bodega**, see ⑪⑥.

After your meal, take a walk around **Bangsar Baru**. Shoppers will love the upmarket **Bangsar Village** (tel: 03-2282 1808; daily 8.30am–10pm) and the **Bangsar Village II** extension on Jalan Telawi 1 (daily 10.30am–10.30pm), with trendy boutiques, cafés and restaurants. At the northern end

of Jalan Maarof, 2km (1½ miles) away, is the **Bangsar Shopping Centre** (tel: 03-2094 7700; daily 10am–10pm).

On Sunday evenings, the stalls of the Bangsar **night market** *(pasar malam)* take over the streets near Bangsar Village. Locals from the neighbourhood come to shop for everything from fresh produce to pirated CDs to plastic toys. But this is upmarket Bangsar after all, so you will find genuine designer brand items amid the clutter of knock-offs.

Above from far left: Royal Malaysian Police Museum armoured tank on display; Mid Valley Megamall; browsing at the Bangsar Night Market.

Food and Drink 🍴

④ **MUSEUM RESTAURANT**
Islamic Arts Museum Malaysia, Jalan Lembah Perdana; tel: 03-2270 5152; Tue–Sun 10am–6pm; $$$
The sumptuous surroundings here are the work of Moroccan craftsmen. Try the sweet baklava or the *meze* combination of Middle Eastern appetisers. For something a little more substantial, opt for the Moroccan lamb *tagine* or grilled chicken with *tahini*.

⑤ **ALEXIS BISTRO**
29 Jalan Telawi 3, Bangsar Baru; tel: 03-2284 2880; www.alexis. com.my; daily 9am–midnight; $$
Famous for its spicy Sarawak *laksa* noodles, Alexis also serves good Napoletana and Margherita pizzas, and fish and chips.

⑥ **LA BODEGA**
16 Jalan Telawi 2, Bangsar Baru; tel: 03-2287 8318; www.bodega. com.my; Mon–Fri noon–1am, Sat–Sun 11am–1am; $$
Its speciality tapas include prawns *a la Andalusia*, grilled lamb cutlets with garlic mayonnaise, and lobster and prawn croquettes. It has an excellent wine list.

Mid Valley and Hartamas

Bangsar is close to two other good entertainment areas. About 2km (1½ miles) south is the Mid Valley City, comprising the huge, popular Mid Valley Megamall (tel: 03-2938 3333; daily 10am–10pm) and its sophisticated high-end sister, The Gardens (tel: 03-2297 0288; daily 10am–10pm), as well as hotels and office towers. The malls are anchored by a cinema chain and Metrojaya, Jusco and Robinson's department stores. This area is accessible via KTM Komuter. Northwest of Bangsar is Desa Sri Hartamas, which, like Bangsar, is an affluent residential area with a commercial centre dominated by restaurants and bars. These include Souled Out, a popular outdoor sports bar, (20 Jalan 30/70A; tel: 03-2300 1955), The Backyard Pub (28 Sri Hartamas 8; tel: 03-6201 0318) and the R&B club Karma Hartamas (1 Jalan 22A/70A; tel: 03-6203 2111). You will need to hire a taxi to get there.

BRICKFIELDS

Explore an old-world KL neighbourhood that, despite its obvious Indian character, is also home to a lively multiracial community and diverse faiths. You will be hard-pressed to find a place like it elsewhere in the city today.

DISTANCE 3½km (2 miles)
TIME Half a day
START Sri Kandaswamy Kovil
END Jalan Tun Sambanthan
POINTS TO NOTE

This is a walking tour best done in the morning or evening to coincide with Hindu prayer times. Take the Monorail to the Tun Sambanthan stop. Walk along Jalan Tebing for about 500m/yd to the Sri Kandaswamy Kovil.

Below: Indian food served on banana leaf in Brickfields.

In the shadow of the ultra-modern transport hub of KL Sentral spreads **Brickfields**, a salt-of-the-earth neighbourhood that dates back to the 19th century, and represents a rapidly vanishing facet of KL. As the city marches towards the national goal of achieving developed-nation status by 2020, government land parcels, such as the northern section of Brickfields, are the first to experience 'urban regeneration'. The area is now KL Sentral.

Development

In the late 19th century, the shanty-town of early KL, with its wooden buildings, was very susceptible to fire. This led the colonial administration to decree that only brick structures were to be built. As its name suggests, Brickfields was where the bricks to rebuild KL were manufactured, and the KL Sentral site was once a clay pit. Later, the latter served as a railway marshalling yard, where train wagons were detached and goods were loaded before the wagons were put together again for the onward journey.

Because of its proximity to KL town, Brickfields also became the site for housing railway and other government employees. Subsequently, a large number of schools and different religious buildings were erected.

SRI KANDASWAMY KOVIL

Brickfields was originally populated by mainly Tamils from southern India and Sri Lanka, who were brought to KL by the British to work in the Malayan Railways and the Public Works Department. Even today, Brickfields retains a very strong Indian character. Your first stop is at the end of Jalan Tebing, facing Jalan Scott. Here stands the **Sri Kandaswamy Kovil** ❶ (tel: 03-2274 2987; www.srikandaswamy kovil.org; daily 5am–1pm and 5–9pm; free), a temple founded by the local Jaffna Sri Lankan community in 1909. The building, reconstructed in 1997, has a tall, elaborate *gopuram* (gateway). The key deity here is Lord Murugan, although the Mother Goddess Sri Raja Rajeswary, who is worshipped as the embodiment of love and grace and rarely found in similar Murugan temples, is also honoured here.

ARULMEGU SREE VEERA HANUMAN TEMPLE

From the Sri Kandaswamy Kovil, continue on Jalan Scott, where Brickfields first took shape. In the early days, the road was filled with Chinese shops, Indian laundries, Chettier moneylenders, and spice and grocery shops that catered to the largely Indian population. At the Lorong Padang Belia junction, on your right is the humble **Arulmegu Sree Veera Hanuman Temple** ❷ (tel: 03-2274 0639; daily 7am–10pm; free), which honours Hanuman, the Monkey God, a deity

not commonly seen in Hindu temples. Depicted in the Indian epic *Ramayana*, Hanuman is revered for his courage and devotion. The temple houses five statues of the deity, which are worshipped with offerings of butter, applied to the mouth and tail, and garlands of *vadai*, a savoury fried fritter.

WEI-LING GALLERY

Further along Jalan Scott, located in a shophouse at no. 8 on your left, is the **Wei-Ling Gallery** ❸ (tel: 03-2260 1106; Mon–Fri noon–7pm, Sat 10am–5pm), a sophisticated, award-winning space that employs a wonderful mix of timber and natural light. Contemporary local and international art is exhibited here. Gutted by fire in 2004, the shophouse was artfully renovated by its previous owner, the renowned architect Jimmy Lim, for his artist daughter, Wei-Ling, who now runs the gallery.

Above from far left: KL Sentral concourse; decorative details at the Sri Kandaswamy Kovil.

Above: flower offerings at the Arulmegu Sree Veera Hanuman Temple; deity in the Sri Kandaswamy Kovil.

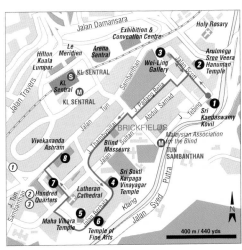

JALAN THAMBYPILLAI

Backtrack along Jalan Scott and turn right onto Lorong Padang Belia. At the end of the road, turn right again and then left onto Jalan Padang Belia. The road skirts a football field that was once a clay pit and now awaits redevelopment. After about 500m/yd is a junction, which is hugged by the YMCA. Turn right and then left onto **Jalan Thambypillai**. This section of Brickfields is perceptibly busier. A notable feature is the large number of blind people on the streets; they frequent the Malaysian Association of the Blind next to the Tun Sambanthan Monorail station. Some are trained masseurs who work in the **massage parlours** on the right side of Jalan Thambypillay. Opposite the massage parlours, interestingly located next to a Buddhist temple, is a red-light district.

JALAN BERHALA

Continue on Jalan Thambypillai till you reach the end, then turn left. At the junction, turn onto **Jalan Berhala** on your left. This U-shaped road, formerly known as Temple Road, is packed with pre-World War II places of worship and a host of schools and bungalows. Take some time to explore its nooks and soak up the atmosphere.

SRI SAKTI KARPAGA VINAYAGAR TEMPLE

A key temple on Jalan Berhala is the **Sri Sakti Karpaga Vinayagar Temple**

➍ (tel: 03-32274 8624; daily 6am–noon and 6–9.30pm, 6am–9.30pm during festivals; free). It is the country's only temple that hosts the Elephant God Vinayagar, also known as Ganesha, who holds a *sivalingam*, the symbol synonymous with the principal god Siva. This is a rare double-deity temple. In the Tamil month of Aavani, from August to September, Vinayagar Sathurthi, the festival honouring the Elephant God, is celebrated with morning prayers at the temple, followed by a parade of this statue in a chariot around Brickfields. The chariot is usually drawn by elephants, and both the deity and the animals are warmly greeted by the local community.

MAHA VIHARA TEMPLE

Where Jalan Berhala curves again stands one of KL's most important Buddhist temples, the **Maha Vihara Temple** ➎ (tel: 03-2274 1141; www.buddhistmahavihara.com; daily 5.30am–10.30pm; free). The temple was founded by the Singhalese who were brought to the Malay peninsula by the British to be civil servants. Temple devotees now include many non-Singhalese but all follow the Sri Lankan Theravada Buddhist faith. Modest in appearance and character on normal days, the temple assumes an electrifying atmosphere on Wesak Day in May. It is the start and end point of a night-time float procession that marks the birth, enlightenment and death of Buddha.

Above from far left: the unpretentious Maha Vihara Temple; deities at Sri Sakti Karpaga Vinayagar Temple; at the night market; Hundred Quarters is steeped in history.

TEMPLE OF FINE ARTS

Just opposite the Maha Vihara's main entrance is the home of the **Temple of Fine Arts** ❻ (tel: 03-2274 3709), where you might hear the sound of ankle bells and tablas. This Indian cultural association has trained young Malaysians in traditional Indian dance and music, including some of the country's top performers. The association is not open to tourists, but it holds shows in theatres around town from time to time. Check local listings or call the association.

HUNDRED QUARTERS

When you reach the end of Jalan Berhala, cross Jalan Sultan Abdul Samad to Jalan Chan Ah Tong. This leads to the **Hundred Quarters** ❼, a Brickfields landmark. Set in rows along both this road and the parallel Jalan Rozario, these 1915 British-built quarters were built of concrete, then considered a luxury, and were among the first that housed civil servants of different ethnic backgrounds. Almost unchanged till today, these buildings continue to host a lively multiethnic community of government employees.

VIVEKANANDA ASHRAM

Standing on Jalan Rozario, you see the **Vivekananda Ashram** ❽, a long pink-and-white building fronting Jalan Tun Sambanthan, established for followers of the influential Indian spiritual leader of the Vedanta branch of Hindu philosophy, which is based on the most speculative and philosophical of Hindu scriptures. Walk to the front of this lovely colonial building to see a statue of Vivekananda.

From Vivekananda Ashram, head left along Jalan Tun Sambanthan. Brickfield's Indian character is most evident here. Shops offer everything from carnatic music to Indian food. **Vischalachirs**, see ⑪①, and **Sri Paandi**, see ⑪②, serve South Indian banana leaf meals. Alternatively, for Chinese fare, try the **New Lay Sin Coffee Shop**, see ⑪③.

Orthodox Church

Among the numerous places of worship in Brickfields is the St Mary's Orthodox Syrian Cathedral (tel: 03-2273 2619; www.mymalankara.com; daily 9am–7pm; free) on Jalan Tun Sambanthan Satu. The faith has its origins in Kerala, and in 1958, the church became the first Orthodox Syrian church to be consecrated outside India. Its most distinguished visitor was the Orthodox Christian Emperor Haile Selassie of Ethiopia, who stopped here during his official visit to Malaysia in 1968, a traffic-stopping event, to say the least.

Food and Drink

① VISCHALACHIRS

19 Jalan Travers; tel: 03-2274 6819; daily 11am–10.45pm; $

This Chettiar family-run restaurant serves excellent traditional meals that are subtle blends of sweet, sour and spicy. Try the rice with *sambar* (stew made from pulses) and *puli kulambu* (tamarind curry), and end with the sweet *payasam* (pudding).

② SRI PAANDI

254 Jalan Tun Sambanthan; tel: 03-2274 0464; 24 hours; $

Typical South Indian dishes, such as chicken *varuval*, mutton curry and deep-fried mackerel to go with Indian bread or steamed rice, served on a banana leaf or metal *thali*.

③ NEW LAY SIN COFFEE SHOP

250 Jalan Tun Sambanthan; no phone; daily 7.30am–2.30pm; $

For 30 years, a stall in this coffee shop has been serving hearty noodles, which come in soup or soy-based variations, with pork, egg and vegetables.

KAMPUNG BARU & JALAN TUANKU ABDUL RAHMAN

Although it sits on prime urban space, Kampung Baru, the city's oldest Malay settlement, has resisted redevelopment and retains a strong traditional Muslim atmosphere. South of it is the historic Jalan Tuanku Abdul Rahman, KL's wholesale and retail fabric centre.

Kampung Baru Mosque

The original site of the 13 May 1969 racial clashes continues to be the venue of politically motivated protests. These include the protest after the 1997 sacking of the Deputy Prime Minister Anwar Ibrahim, and another against the publication of caricatures of the Prophet Muhamad in a Danish newspaper in 2005.

DISTANCE 6km (3¾ miles)

TIME Half a day

START No. 60 Jalan Raja Muda Musa

END Lebuh Ampang

POINTS TO NOTE

Take the LRT to the Kampung Baru station. When you leave the station, turn left onto Jalan Sungai Baharu and right onto Jalan Raja Muda Musa. About 100m/yd on your right is the hawker centre, where your tour begins. Time your tour so you have a meal at the Coliseum Café. Dress conservatively to do this tour, since you are exploring a Muslim enclave.

This tour takes you around two old areas. Kampung Baru has always resisted the kind of large-scale redevelopment that has taken over much of KL's city centre. Conversely, while Jalan Tuanku Abdul Rahman has always embraced change, its traditional textile businesses have survived till this day.

KAMPUNG BARU

Kampung Baru means 'new village' in Malay. It was established in the late 1890s by the British to address the problem of the declining Malay population in KL. The colonials' plan was to encourage Malays to participate in its administration and enjoy the prosperity that living in KL could bring.

Today, many of the original wooden houses have been replaced by brick structures and high-rise buildings, but the area remains distinctively Malay. Doorways are adorned with the *asalamualaikum* welcome sign in Jawi, and children in traditional dress make their way to or from religious classes.

Because of the area's majority Muslim population, a large part of which are in fact Indonesian, particularly Javanese, the Ramadan fasting

Food and Drink

① JALAN RAJA MUDA MUSA HAWKER CENTRE

Jalan Raja Muda Musa; daily 6.30am–1am; $

The stalls here are good for Malay specialities such as *nasi lemak* (coconut rice), *lontong* (rice cakes with coconut gravy) and the East Coast regional favourite, *nasi kerabu* (herbed rice salad).

② RESTORAN MAJU GARUDA

36B Jalan Raja Alang; tel: 03-2691 4077; daily 7am–midnight; $

A rustic *minang* (Indonesian) restaurant serving traditional *nasi padang* (rice with side dishes). Try the *ayam pop* (deep-fried chicken), crispy beef *dendeng* and the oxtail soup.

month is a particularly good time to go on this tour. Come here just before the breaking of fast at sunset, when the streets are lined with food stalls of the **Pasar Ramadan** (3pm–midnight), offering delicacies that are prepared only during this period.

Jalan Raja Alang

Start with breakfast at the **hawker centre**, see ⑪①, where you can find a nice selection of home-cooked Malay food. From the hawker centre, walk along Jalan Raja Alang. Traditional wooden Malay architecture may be fast disappearing in this city, but **no. 60 ❶** is an illustrative example, despite being painted a garish green. This grand Malay house has a raised central *serambi* reception area fronted by ceiling-to-floor windows for ventilation and flanked by two curving stairways. The spacious front yard now serves as a food stall; this is common in Kampung Baru. As you continue along Jalan Raja Alang, note how the other houses on this road have retained parts of their original structures while adopting modern trappings.

Kampung Baru Mosque

Further along Jalan Raja Alang is **Masjid Kampung Baru ❷** (Kampung Baru Mosque; daily 9am–5pm, except prayer times) on your right. Built around 1924, it was one of the first concrete structures in the quarter. Its new gateway is adorned with a turquoise ceramic pattern, similar to that of the Islamic Arts Museum *(see p.48)*, which is of Middle Eastern origins.

Guru Nanak Darbaar Gurdwara Sahib

Cross Jalan Raja Abdullah and continue along Jalan Raja Alang. You pass **Restoran Maju Garuda**, see ⑪②, an Indonesian restaurant. After 200m/yd is an impressive domed building, on your right. This is the **Guru Nanak Darbaar Gurdwara Sahib ❸**. This Sikh temple is only open to worshippers, so admire it from the outside. Of note are its pumpkin-shaped Indo-

Above from far left: Muslim school boys; Guru Nanak Darbaar Gurdwara Sahib's pumpkin-shaped dome; Malay house in Kampung Baru.

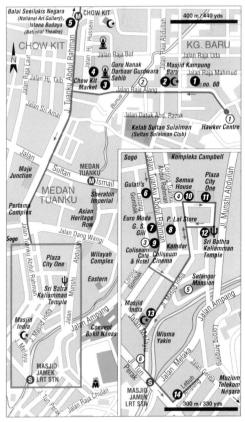

Above from left: street chess in Chow Kit; contemporary art in the National Art Gallery; religious paraphernalia in Jalan Masjid India.

The Longest Road
Jalan Tuanku Abdul Rahman was once KL's longest road. Originally called Batu Road, it led to the tin mines in Batu village. It later became the city's main shopping area and earned the moniker of 'Golden Mile'. In 1963, the name of the road was changed to honour the first *Agong* (king) of the newly formed Malaysia.

Persian domes, adorned at the base with lotus petals. The central dome has a miniature umbrella called a *shatri*, symbolising shelter for mankind. Its main prayer hall is the largest in Southeast Asia.

CHOW KIT MARKET

As you continue along Jalan Raja Alang, you will pass a host of fruit stalls (daily 24 hours) on your right, selling tropical fruits like durian, rambutan and jackfruit. These stalls mark the boundary of the **Chow Kit Market ❹** (daily 6am–8pm), one of the largest and oldest traditional fresh-produce markets in the city. Walk in through any of passageways through the fruit stalls. Be warned that the alleyways are damp, congested and strong-smelling. You can find spices and herbs used in Malay cooking, cooked food as well as fish, meat, vegetables and sundries.

NATIONAL ART GALLERY

From Chow Kit Market, you may want to take a 10-minute taxi ride north to check out the **National Art Gallery ❺** (Balai Senilukis Negara; tel: 03-4025 4990; www.artgallery.gov.my; daily 10am–6pm; free). Five galleries are housed in an elegant, multistorey contemporary space. The main gallery on the ground floor showcases works from the 2,500-piece permanent collection. There are new exhibitions every three months.

Next to the gallery is a less successful architectural structure, **Istana Budaya** (National Theatre; tel: 03-4026 0555; www.istanabudaya.gov.my). Looking like an oversized Malay house, the theatre hosts large-scale local and international productions. Each Saturday night, the car park hosts the colourful **Laman Santai** (8pm–midnight), with arts and craft stalls and traditional performances.

Right: seafood and fresh produce at the Chow Kit Market.

JALAN TUANKU ABDUL RAHMAN

If you forgo the National Art Gallery, take a taxi along **Jalan Tuanku Abdul Rahman** to the **Sogo** shopping complex, 1 km (½ mile) south. You could walk there but the sights along the way are not very interesting. This is the starting point for exploring what was once the main shopping drag of the colonial capital. Today, it is KL's Garment District. From Sogo, walk south along Jalan Tuanku Abdul Rahman, keeping to the right-hand side.

It is fabrics galore on Jalan Tuanku Abdul Rahman. Wholesale and retail shops trade in all manner of textiles, from knitted to felt and local to imported, in the shape of bales or clothing. The silk market is dominated by **Gulati's ⑥** (no. 162/164; tel: 03-2698 3901; Mon–Fri 10.30am–8.30pm, Sat 10.30am–9pm, Sun 11am–9pm) on your right. The same Sikh-owned company also operates the poshest fabric house in town, **Euro Moda**, further down the road (no. 126/128; tel: 03-2694 0805; daily 10am–8.30pm). There are fabrics and garments from India, France and Italy. This is also where you are most likely to spot high-society Mak Datins (wealthy, older Malay women), starlets and politicians' wives receiving personalised service and seeking design and tailoring consultation.

Continue along the road till you come to no. 106, **G.S. Gill ⑦** (tel: 03-2698 3477; Mon–Fri 9.30am–6.30pm, Sat 10am–6pm, Sun 10am–5pm). The sports store is a wholesaler that also makes its own footballs, racquets and export-quality golf gear. Opposite it at no. 135 is **P. Lal Store ⑧** (tel: 03-2694 2694; Mon–Sat 10am–7pm), now a third-generation business, selling mainly high-end leather shoes, tobacco pipes and winter clothing imported from the UK.

Both shops were set up in the late-19th or early-20th century and are testament to the remarkable lasting power of multi-generational family businesses that dominate this street. Like many other businesses here, these were established by businessmen from the Indian subcontinent.

Tailoring

Many locals still tailor their outfits. Jalan Tuanku Abdul Rahman is filled with tailors whose forte is traditional ethnic outfits. Several among them can make Western-style outfits at reasonable prices; some offer 24-hour turnaround time.

Textile Currency

Indian textiles were the currency of 15th- and 16th-century trade in the region. The textiles were brought to the Malay isles by Indian traders, who were mostly from Gujarat. The Indian producers also adapted their designs and styles to cater to local tastes and traditions. The two cloths that dominated the textile markets were chintz – both fine and coarse painted and dyed cottons – and *patola*, the Gujarati double-*ikat* silk cloth that also symbolised wealth. Today, India continues to be a major source of fabrics sold in Jalan Tuanku Abdul Rahman and Jalan Masjid India.

Mehndi
The application of henna designs called *mehndi* (Indian) or *berinai* (Malay) on newly-weds is to bring good luck; this sometimes involves the mother-in-law who paints the first dot to indicate her blessing. Now it is done anytime for fun.

THE COLISEUM

It should be time for lunch now. A couple of doors from G.S. Gill is the **Coliseum Café**, see ⑪③, renowned for its sizzling steaks and baked crab, white tablecloths and napkins yellowed with age, and the few remaining Hainanese Chinese waitstaff whose forefathers once cooked for the colonials. Built in 1928, the **Coliseum Café and Hotel** ❾ (tel: 03-2692 6270; daily 10am–10pm) has definitely seen better days, but its original decor and mismatched furniture and fittings are quaintly nostalgic. Its bar, now frequented by lawyers and tourists, was once a popular drinking hole for prosperous colonial planters, tin miners and traders. Next door is the **Coliseum Cinema**, one of the city's last remaining traditional cinemas, with its noteworthy neoclassical architectural features. Today, it screens mainly Malay, Tamil and Indonesian movies.

MASJID INDIA

Cross the road at the pedestrian crossing and take Lorong Tuanku Abdul Rahman 3 on the right to get to **Jalan Masjid India**, which runs parallel to Jalan Tuanku Abdul Rahman. Formerly sporting a marked Indian Muslim accent, it is becoming increasingly Malay today. Its every available space is taken up by shops, restaurants and colourful pavement stalls. There are Malay outfits, scarves and sarongs as well as Indian clothing and shoes, while elaborate gold jewellery glitters in its window displays.

Jalan Masjid India ends at a shopping mall called **Semua House** ❿ (tel: 03-2693 5899; daily 10am–8pm), a one-stop shop for Malay weddings, with everything from fabrics and artificial flowers to gift baskets and costume rentals. It also has several eateries such as **Sagar Café**, see ⑪④.

To its right, **Plaza City One** ⓫ (daily 9am–10pm) is a high-rise Little India, with jewellery, traditional and Bollywood-style clothing, and *mehndi* (henna-painting) services. From here, walk to the end of the street, turn right and go through the carpark. Ahead, beneath the spreading branches of a

---

Food and Drink

③ COLISEUM CAFÉ
98–100 Jalan Tuanku Abdul Rahman; tel: 03-2692 6270; daily 10am–10pm, Sun from 9am; $
Revisit the colonial days at this famous café. Try a gunner, then have a sizzling ribeye or baked crabmeat with salad. There are also firewood-baked English pot pies.

④ SAGAR CAFÉ
G/F, Semua House; Lorong Bunus 6; daily 8am–8pm; $
Enjoy an alfresco meal at this trendy, self-service outlet operated by an old tandoori iconic restaurant. The naan, chicken and dhal dishes are good.

⑤ SARAVANAA BHAVAN
1007 Selangor Mansion, Jalan Masjid India; tel: 03-2287 1228; daily 8.30am–11pm; $
Excellent Indian vegetarian food. The must-tries are the chilli *paneer* (spicy fried cottage cheese), cauliflower Manchuria and mushroom *roghan josh*.

⑥ O'BRIEN'S
G/F, Menara OCBC, 18 Jalan Tun Perak; tel: 03-2698 2281; Mon–Sat 7am–8pm; $
Freshly made sandwiches from an eclectic menu with choices like toasted Crambo Club Tootsie with turkey ham, bacon and cheese. The café also has great gourmet coffee and fresh juices.

century-old fig tree, is a tiny Hindu temple, **Sri Bathra Kaliamman Temple** ⑫ (daily 6am–10pm). Its main deity is the green-faced Kali the Destroyer. Note the cobra-shaped worship paraphernalia in front of the temple; these are to appease an ancient cobra said to inhabit the fig tree.

From the temple, turn left and walk down Lorong Bunus 5 and turn left at the junction to Jalan Masjid India. Walk down this road; on your left behind the hawker centre is Selangor Mansion where you will find an excellent vegetarian restaurant, **Saravanaa Bhavan**, see ⑪⑤. Continue along Jalan Masjid India until you reach a covered area, the **Masjid India Bazaar**.

To your right is the brown-slate-covered **Masjid India** ⑬, a 19th-century Indian Muslim mosque after which the street is named. Here, prayers are conducted in Arabic and Tamil. Although the mosque is open only to Muslim worshippers, do linger to appreciate its Indian Muslim atmosphere. On Fridays, the entire bazaar area outside the mosque is filled with worshippers and shoppers buying Malay and Islamic knick-knacks. There are good photo opportunities here, but do be discreet and respect the worshippers' right to privacy.

Opposite the mosque, to the left of the bazaar, is **Wisma Yakin** (daily 9am–9.30pm), an emporium of Malay shops where you can buy good local and Indonesian batik, traditional herbal concoctions for health and beauty, and other Malay goods. Walk through the bazaar and reach Jalan Melayu. On your right is Menara OCBC, where you can enjoy a sandwich at **O'Brien's**, see ⑪⑥. Otherwise, turn left and, at the Masjid Jamek LRT Station, turn left again onto Jalan Tun Perak.

LEBUH AMPANG

Walk along Jalan Tun Perak and turn left onto **Lebuh Ampang** ⑭. This is where Indian Chettiar money-lenders once ruled the street and funded many local economic activities before World War II. Though the chettiars are no longer around, the rows of early 20th-century shophouses here have been left largely intact, complete with Greek columns, moulded plaster decorations and roof-level parapets. The area still has a distinctly Indian feel. Several shops deal in Indian-style filigree 22-karat gold; others sell household goods, religious paraphernalia and music CDs.

Left: Indian jewellery.

Above from far left: bar at the Coliseum; fabrics in Jalan Masjid India; old-style barber.

Telecommunications Museum
On the corner of Jalan Gereja and Jalan Raja Chulan is one of the finest examples of KL's Western classical-style buildings. Built in 1928, the building now houses the Muzium Telekom Negara (National Telecommunications Museum; tel: 03-2026 7967; Tue–Sun 9am–5pm). Its exhibits are unimpressive but the structure stands out for its magnificent, symmetrical neo-classical features.

MASJID INDIA **59**

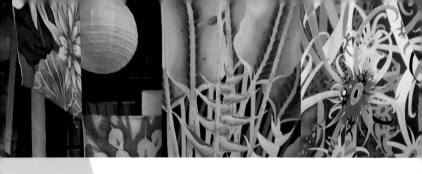

BUKIT BINTANG

In the city's main commercial district, shopping malls, chic boutiques, craft and heritage centres, acclaimed restaurants and nightlife venues vie for your attention. Find just about anything you desire in this bustling zone.

DISTANCE 5km (3 miles)
TIME Half a day
START Kompleks Kraf
END Changkat Bukit Bintang
POINTS TO NOTE
This tour is recommended as an afternoon-to-evening itinerary, but start earlier if you enjoy shopping. To get to the Kompleks Kraf, take a taxi or walk from the KLCC LRT station.

Craft Festival
Each year at the end of February or in early March, the Kompleks Kraf Kuala Lumpur hosts a week-long festival of handicrafts from all over Malaysia. Besides the sale of products and craft demonstrations, there are also cultural performances. Call the centre for details.

Bukit Bintang has the largest number of malls, restaurants and hotels per square metre in the city. Its retail offerings will satisfy even the most fanatic of shopaholics, while those less keen on shopping will have a plethora of tourist sights, craft centres, cafés, restaurants and watering holes to choose from.

CRAFT COMPLEX

Begin at the **Kompleks Kraf Kuala Lumpur** ❶ (Kuala Lumpur Craft Complex; tel: 03-2162 7459; daily 9am–8pm; free) on Jalan Conlay. This one-stop craft centre, a more upmarket version of the Central Market *(see p.33)*, is particularly rewarding for souvenir hunters, with quality Malaysian

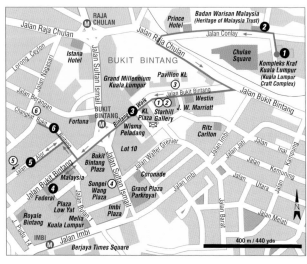

arts and crafts. Besides a souvenir shop, cafeteria and a **craft museum** (daily 9am–5.30pm; charge), the complex also houses an **Artists' Colony** (daily 10am–6pm; free), a cluster of 22 huts where a number of up-and-coming Malaysian artists work on their art and conduct classes for visitors. Most of their works are for sale.

BADAN WARISAN

From Kompleks Kraf, walk along Jalan Conlay towards Jalan Raja Chulan. At the junction of Jalan Stonor sits a 1925 bungalow that houses the **Badan Warisan Malaysia ❷** (Heritage of Malaysia Trust; tel: 03-2144 9373; www.badanwarisan.org.my; Mon–Sat 10am–5.30pm; free). This non-governmental organisation advocates the preservation and conservation of the country's built heritage.

Headman's House
A highlight is the **Rumah Penghulu Abu Seman** (tours Mon–Sat 11am and 3pm; charge), a beautiful traditional Malay timber house relocated from the northern state of Kedah. Formerly a headman's house, it was restored as an awareness-raising project. In the grounds as well is a resource centre (Tue–Sat 10am–4pm by appointment; charge) and a gift shop with a range of cards and collectibles.

BINTANG WALK

From Badan Warisan, continue on Jalan Conlay and turn left onto Jalan Raja Chulan at the junction. Cross the road to get to **Jalan Bukit Bintang**. Stretching beside the thoroughfare from the Westin hotel to the Lot 10 mall is a wide pedestrian mall known as **Bintang Walk ❸**. Lined with boutiques, cafés and restaurants, it is a great spot to relax and people-watch.

Starhill Gallery
From the Westin, walk past the J.W. Marriott hotel and get to the sophisticated **Starhill Gallery** (tel: 03-2148 1000; www.starhillgallery.com; daily 10am–9.30pm). A favourite of the well-heeled, it features boutiques of high-end brands such as Louis Vuitton and Dior, an entire floor dedicated to art galleries, and a basement Feast Village with some of KL's most acclaimed restaurants, such as **Shook!**, see ⑪①, and **Enak**, see ⑪②.

Pavilion Kuala Lumpur
Opposite Starhill Gallery is another ritzy mall, the mammoth 450-outlet **Pavilion Kuala Lumpur** (tel: 03-2143

Above from far left: batik art; Shook! restaurant.

Traffic Jams
The bane of taxi drivers, Bukit Bintang has become a traffic nightmare both day and night, so use public transport to get there.

Food and Drink 🍴

① SHOOK!
Feast Village, Starhill Gallery; tel: 03-2719 8535; daily noon–1am; $$$
In a beautiful open dining area with four show kitchens, chefs put together Japanese, Chinese, Italian and Western selections.

② ENAK
Feast Village, Starhill Gallery; tel: 03-2141 8973; daily noon–midnight; $$$
Malay cuisine in an elegant setting. Try the king prawns simmered in a creamy coconut milk sauce and slow-cooked beef with spices and herbs. For dessert, the young coconut custard meringue is a good choice.

8088; www.pavilion-kl.com; daily 10am–10pm). Connected via a long walkway to the Kuala Lumpur Convention Centre, Pavilion hosts concept stores and entertainment outlets. Its Japanese-style bistro, **The Loaf**, see 🍴③, is a good refreshment stop.

More Malls

Bukit Bintang's malls offer all kinds of goods, from books and IT products to cameras. But its real draw is fashion; prices for haute couture designer wear and Malaysian-designed apparel and other accessories are very reasonable.

Located next to Starhill Gallery is **Kuala Lumpur Plaza** (tel: 03-2141 7288; daily 11am–10pm), with a **Planet Hollywood** outlet (tel: 03-2144 6602; Sun–Thur 11.30am–2.30am, Fri–Sat 11.30am–3am). Also worth a look here is **Bernard Chandran**'s boutique (tel: 03-2145 0534; Mon–Fri 9am–6pm, Sat 9am–2pm), one of Malaysia's most talented couturiers. Further along is **Lot 10**, a green monolith with fashionable boutiques and the Japanese department store **Isetan**.

Across from Lot 10 on Jalan Sultan Ismail is **Sungei Wang Plaza** (tel: 03-2148 6109; daily 10am–10pm). Besides hosting boutiques of Malaysian fashion designers such as Zang Toi and Melinda Looi, the mall is also the stomping ground of KL's young, trend-conscious set, who trawl its shops for the unusual and new. A good dining spot here is **Esquire Kitchen**, see 🍴④.

If you hanker for even more shopping, there is also **Berjaya Times Square** (tel: 03-2144 9821; www.timessquarekl.com; daily 10am–10pm), the city's largest mall with 900 outlets, on Jalan Imbi. A self-contained entertainment city, it also has a cineplex, IMAX theatre and the indoor theme park Cosmo's.

Below right:
indoor Theme Park, Cosmo's, in Berjaya Times Square.

Food and Drink 🍴

③ THE LOAF
Lot 3.13.00 & 4.12.02, Level 3 & 4, Pavilion Kuala Lumpur; tel: 03-2145 3036; daily 10am–10pm; $$
This bakery-cum-bistro offers healthy Japanese-style breads and pastries, gourmet sandwiches and frozen lattes.

④ ESQUIRE KITCHEN
Level 1, Sungei Wang Plaza; tel: 03-2148 4506; daily 11am–9.30pm; $
A long-time favourite of locals; recommended are the Shanghainese dumplings, noodles and pork dishes.

⑤ NGAU KEE BEEF NOODLES
Tengkat Tong Shin; daily 6pm–2am; $
This 35-year-old roadside stall is famous for its noodles with minced beef served with a hearty soup. The *lo shu fun* (rice noodles) with beef dumplings is also good.

⑥ RELISH
22 Changkat Bukit Bintang; tel: 03-2145 3321; Sun–Thur noon–midnight, Fri–Sat noon–1am; $$
Choose from chicken, beef and vegetarian gourmet burgers. Try the hearty Aussie Burger or the Lamb Minty in a pita pocket.

THE FEDERAL

If you continue down Jalan Bukit Bintang, you come to **The Federal ❹** (tel: 03-2148 9166; www.federal.com.my), at no. 35. Built at the request of the first prime minister Tunku Abdul Rahman to house visiting dignitaries, the hotel was completed just three days before Malaya achieved independence on 31 August 1957. Its revolving restaurant, the only one in the city, remains popular today. Behind the hotel, **Plaza Low Yat** (tel: 03-2148 3651; daily 10am–10pm) offers bargain computer products.

JALAN ALOR

If it is time for dinner, cross Jalan Bukit Bintang and go up Changkat Bukit Bintang, Turn left into **Jalan Alor ❺**. The street transforms from congested chaos in the day into a brightly lit outdoor dining hub at night, with stalls selling a wide range of street food, from barbecued wings to grilled seafood. On **Tengkat Tong Shin**, the next street parallel to Jalan Alor, is the famous, no-frills **Ngau Kee Beef Noodles** stall, see ⑪⑤.

CHANGKAT BUKIT BINTANG

For more dinner choices, turn left at the junction of Jalan Alor and Changkat Bukit Bintang. Among the eateries here is **Relish**, see ⑪⑥, a smart gourmet-burger joint.

Changkat Bukit Bintang ❻, once a seedy neighbourhood, is now filled with watering holes and a cluster of 'flashpackers', higher-end backpacker accommodation, all housed in classy refurbished pre-war shophouses.

After dinner, explore the nightlife options of Changkat Bukit Bintang. Among the nightlife gems here are the Japanese jazz club **Yoko's** (tel: 03-2144 3387), the chic gay bar **Frangipani** (tel: 03-2144 3001), and **Little Havana** (tel: 03-2144 7170), with Latin music and dancing. On Jalan Mesui is **No Black Tie** (tel: 03-2142 3737), which features live-music performances.

Above from far left: Zang Toi boutique in Lot 10 mall; bustling Jalan Bukit Bintang; a 'flash-packer' in Changkat Bukit Bintang; gay hotspot Frangipani.

Urban Renewal

The original entertainment quarter of the 1950s, Bukit Bintang ('Star Hill') had become overwhelmed by congestion, grime and vice 30 years later. At the turn of the century, it was rescued by real estate giant YTL, which spent millions of ringgit in a property buyout and in building Bintang Walk, the pedestrian mall fashioned after the Avenue des Champs-Elysées in Paris. Unfortunately, change came at a cost – an architecturally important century-old girls' school was demolished to make way for the mega Pavilion Kuala Lumpur mall. Many of the original residents in the back lanes have also moved out and migrant workers have taken over the housing. Prostitution, once rampant in the area, still exists, although pushed to the fringes.

BATU CAVES

The Batu Caves are home to a beautiful temple, one of the most important for Kuala Lumpur Hindus, and well worth the climb up the limestone massif. At its base are other shrines and galleries of traditional Indian art.

DISTANCE The Batu Caves are 13km (8 miles) from KL; the tour itself covers 4km (2½ miles)

TIME 3 hours

START Nadarajar Hall

END Velluvar Kottem

POINTS TO NOTE

Take a taxi from the city (½ hour; RM15 one way). Most outer city tours also include the Batu Caves. Make arrangements with your hotel tour desk.

Free Entry

Do not fall prey to requests for entrance fees to the shrines. Admission to all shrines is free; fees apply only to the art galleries.

Cave Ecology

The Batu Caves Temple complex, which supports a fragile, unique ecosystem, is also of interest to cave ecologists and geologists. It is the southernmost limestone outcrop in the Northern Hemisphere. Visit the Dark Caves, a 2-km (1¼-mile) long chamber, to explore its ecosystem; book with the Malaysian Nature Society (mobile tel: 012-310 3464; charge).

No visit to KL is complete without a trip to the **Batu Caves**. The Batu Caves was a popular picnic spot for the British during the colonial years before Hindus began to make pilgrimages to the caves. It was officially established as the **Sri Subramaniar Swamy Temple** (tel: 03-6189 6284; office Mon–Fri 9am–5pm) in 1891 by K. Thambusamy Pillai, the founder of the Sri Maha Mariamman Temple on Jalan Tun H.S. Lee in KL *(see p.37)*.

MURUGAN STATUE

At the base of the Batu Caves is a 43-m (140-ft) **gilded statue of Murugan**, the largest of its kind in the world. Hundreds of tonnes of concrete and steel bars and 300 litres (800 gallons) of gold paint were used to create the statue. In the **Nadarajar Hall**, in the car park, you can watch a 15-minute documentary (mobile tel: 016-6983 385; daily 9am–5.30pm; charge) on the temple, Thaipusam festival and the making of the Murugan statue.

TEMPLE CAVE

Behind the statue is the immense 272-step staircase that leads up to the **Temple Cave** (daily 7.30am–1pm and 4–8.30pm, except Thaipusam 24 hours; free). Monkeys perch along the staircase up to the Temple Cave. They can be aggressive, so keep a safe distance and never feed them.

The large Temple Cave, measuring 80 by 100m (260 by 330ft), holds a shrine dedicated to Lord Murugan,

who manifests virtue, valour, youth and vitality, and is known as a destroyer of evil and a dispenser of favours. Worshippers pray to a *vel*, Murugan's trident, which dates back to the temple's beginnings. Other deities are also honoured here.

If there are worshippers at the shrine, do keep a respectful distance. Every year during Thaipusam, over a million devotees gather here to offer thanks and prayers to Murugan (*see below right*).

SHRINES AND GALLERIES

There are other shrines at the base of the Batu Caves. To the left of the steps are shrines that honour the Elephant God Ganesha, Meenatchi Amma and Sivan, and to the right is one dedicated to Saneeswarar.

Located in separate structures about 200m/yd further to the left are shrines to Perumal and Anchaneyar, also known as Hanuman. The latter, the Monkey God, is a key character in the Indian epic *Ramayana* and is represented here by a 15-m (50-ft) tall statue.

You may also want to visit the **Gallery of Indian Art** and **Velluvar Kottem** (both daily 6am–9pm; charge), located to the left of the Ganesha shrine, in separate caves. The former features intricate, bright wall paintings of Indian myths while the Velluvar Kottem has colourful clay figurines.

Restaurants here mainly serve vegetarian Indian meals, see 🍴① and 🍴②.

Above from far left: statue of Lord Murugan welcomes pilgrims to the lime-stone caves; inside the Temple Cave; souvenirs from the cave; devotee seeks blessings.

Food and Drink 🍴

① RANI RESTAURANT
10 Batu Caves Temple; tel: 03-6186 2518; daily 7.30am–9.30pm; $
Serving pure vegetarian and *jain* food (no garlic or onion), this is known for its special *masala* tea (a milky tea infused with spices), excellent with the *masala thosai* (crepes filled with potatoes).

② DHIVYA'S CAFÉ
9 Batu Caves Temple; tel: 03-6185 3788; daily 7am–8pm; $
Order the vegetarian burger, or mock chicken or mutton to go with the banana leaf meal.

Thaipusam

Thaipusam, the Hindu festival of repentance, is a riot of colours, sounds and emotions. It is also a deeply communal event, where devotees fulfil vows, surrounded by family and friends. A statue of Murugan is carried on a silver chariot on a 15-km (9-mile) long journey from the Sri Maha Mariamman Temple on Jalan Tun H.S. Lee in KL to the Batu Caves Temple. Devotees who have had a request granted by Murugan carry milk up to the Temple Cave to bathe his statue. Milk is also transported in large structures called *kavadis*, some of which weigh over 20kg (44lbs). *Kavadi*-carrying, which originates from a myth in which a mountain with Murugan at its apex was lifted, symbolises the willingness to bear burdens. The acts of penance also include the piercing of backs, cheeks, tongues and other body parts.

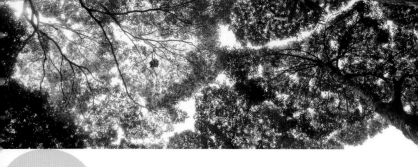

FOREST RESEARCH INSTITUTE OF MALAYSIA

Discover a sprawling tropical rainforest located on the edge of the city. Part of a research institute, the forest holds star attractions such as a canopy walkway and splendid collections of old Malaysian trees.

Above: view from the canopy walkway.

Insectarium
If insects do not creep you out, check out the FRIM Insectarium where you can find an exhibition showcasing the history of insects. Next to it sits a garden of flowering plants that is intended to host insects and their young. Inquire at the Information Centre for more details.

DISTANCE FRIM is 16km (10 miles) northwest of KL; the walk itself covers 6km (3¾ miles)
TIME Half a day or a full day
START AND END FRIM Information Centre
POINTS TO NOTE
This is a half or full-day tour, depending on whether you enjoy being in the forest. The best time to visit is in the early morning or early evening when it is cooler, although the rainforest is usually shady any time of the day. Remember to drink lots of water and wear sturdy walking shoes. There are no direct bus services from KL to FRIM, so hire a taxi for the day (RM20–25 per hour). The closest KTM Komuter station is Kepong, where you can catch a taxi (RM15) to FRIM. Arrange with the taxi driver to pick you up at the end of the tour.

The oldest jungles in the world are the tropical rainforests of Southeast Asia and South America. Looking at the mostly urban KL today, though, it is difficult to believe the city was once covered with dense tropical rainforest. Those who wish to visit a lush rain-forest but do not want to travel too far out can head to the **Forest Research Institute of Malaysia** (FRIM; daily 7am–7pm; www.frim.gov.my; charge), one of the world's oldest forest research centres, opened in 1929.

The Forest

The forest in the 600-ha (1,480-acre) FRIM hosts an incredible variety of flora and fauna. It is not virgin forest, however, but a testament to what can happen if degraded land is left to thrive on its own for over 60 years.

The forest is liveliest in the early morning and late evening, with cicada choruses, chirping crickets and bird calls. Small animals such as squirrels and tree shrews scurry among the branches, and reptiles like lizards and skinks sun themselves on the rocks.

Information Centre

Check in first at the **Information Centre ❶** (tel: 03-6279 7525; daily 9am–4pm, except some public holidays); staff can help you sort out your itinerary. You can also book guided tours by calling ahead. If the Information Centre is closed, the large map of the park trails to the left of the car park is useful.

CANOPY WALKWAY

Register and pay for the Canopy Walkway at the Information Centre. Registration closes at 1pm, but the walkway is open Tue–Thur and Sat–Sun 9.30am–2.30pm. Book ahead during the school holidays. Walk along Jalan FRIM for about 400m/yd and turn right when you see the signpost to the Canopy Walkway. This leads to the 3-km (1¼-mile) **Rover Track ❷**, which winds through tall trees, woody liana creepers and a thick shrub layer. About 1km (½ mile) on is a turn-off to the **Canopy Walkway ❸**. This 500-m/yd section will get your heart pumping, as it climbs steeply up **Bukit Nolang** (489m/1,604ft), where the Canopy Walkway is located.

The Canopy Walkway, made of a secure network of ropes and ladders, was built for scientists to study canopy-level flora and fauna. Anchored to five large trees, it stretches over 200m/yd and suspends up to 30m (100ft) above the forest floor. There are platforms for rest and fantastic views along the walkway. At the canopy level, you can appreciate the multi-canopied structure of the rainforest. Each canopy is a sub-ecosystem on its own, with life forms that are different from those on the forest ground, such as shoots reaching high towards sunlight and insects pollinating flowers.

ARBORETUMS

When you get off the walkway, there are two ways back to the Information Centre. One is to go back the way you came. The other is a 3-km (2-mile) hike that lets you see more of FRIM. On the second route, continue along the trail downhill till you reach the main Rover Track again. Turn right and go past a pretty waterfall. The trail then leaves the forest and joins Jalan Symington, which brings you past the **Dipterocarp Arboretum ❹** and the **Non-Dipterocarp Arboretum ❺**.

There are a total of six arboretums in FRIM, showcasing, among others, indigenous fruit trees, conifers and monocotyledenous trees. The Dipterocarp Arboretum is world-renowned and contains some of the country's oldest and rarest trees, which are widely referenced by scientists. Dipterocarps are the largest tree family in

Above from far left: canopy at FRIM; on the canopy walkway.

Arboretums
These are large, open spaces planted with specific species, usually woody plants, for study and display. Some of FRIM's arboretums were started in 1929 when the institute was established.

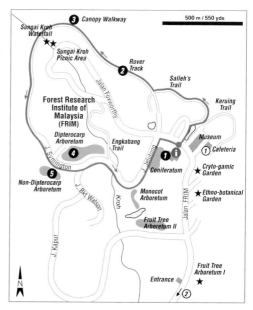

Above from left:
way to the canopy walkway; jogging in FRIM; whitewater kayaking in Kuala Kubu Bharu; Sungai Selangor Dam.

Malaysia, covering almost three-quarters of its natural forested areas.

At the junction, turn left onto Jalan Bukit Watson; this takes you back to the Information Centre.

EASY TRAILS

There are also easier walks to choose from. One option is to follow the paved road as it loops through the grounds. You can also check out the five short nature trails, including the **Keruing**, **Salleh's** and **Engkabang trails**, which are fairly flat and made for easy walking. Ranging 1–1¹⁄₂km (¹⁄₂–1¹⁄₄ miles), the trails take about half an hour each to complete.

MINI SHOWCASES

If you have the time, visit the **Ethno-botanical Garden** (you must book at the Information Centre) on Jalan FRIM. This is a showcase of herbs

Below:
Sungai Kroh.

traditionally used by indigenous and rural people. There is also a **museum** (daily 9am–4pm), near the Information Centre, with informative displays on forestry history and practices in Malaysia, forest products and research activities conducted by FRIM.

SUNGAI KROH

A picnic in the forest is lovely, so buy water and snacks from the **cafeteria**, see 🍴①, or pack a picnic meal from the city. There are several beautiful streams and waterfalls in FRIM; especially popular is the waterfall at **Sungai Kroh**, great for splashing around in during the rainy season from March to May and September to December.

You can camp overnight at the park, but you will need to obtain permission from the park authorities first. After your tour of FRIM, you may want to enjoy a Nonya meal at **Red Door**, see 🍴②, in Kepong.

Food and Drink

① FRIM CAFETERIA
Jalan Foxworthy; daily 9am–7pm; $
Selling mainly Malay fare. Buy drinks and sandwiches for your hike, or have a hot meal here thereafter.

② RED DOOR
Lot F27, 1/F, Jusco Metro Prima Shopping Centre, 1 Jalan Metro Prima, off Jalan Kepong; tel: 03-6252 6186; daily 10am–10.30pm; $
A lovely Nonya eatery with friendly service. Its specialities include chicken curry, fried chicken, 'top hats' (pastry cups) filled with shredded yam bean, and spicy chilli beef.

KUALA KUBU BHARU

A playground for whitewater rafting and other adventure and nature-based activities, Kuala Kubu Bharu and its peaceful surroundings are popular with day-trippers.

Sungai Selangor flows for 110km (67 miles) through the state of Selangor from the Titiwangsa Main Range into the Straits of Malacca near the town of Kuala Selangor. Like many other rivers, it has charted the course of settlements, including that of **Kuala Kubu Bharu ❶**. KKB, as the locals call the town, used to be just another sleepy hollow en route to the highland retreat of Fraser's Hill *(see p.72)*. While the town itself is placid, with simple eateries and grocery shops, it has become a jump-off point for nature activities and adventure sports, thanks to the presence of Sungai Selangor and the surrounding forests.

The town is also an excellent stop before and after outdoor tours for meals and for stocking up supplies. The **Post Office Hawker Stalls**, see ⑪①, are popular for breakfast, while **Restoran Ninety Eight**, see ⑪②, and **Kedai Makanan Govindamah**, see ⑪③, are good for lunch and dinner.

WHITEWATER SPORTS

Sungai Selangor is arguably the top whitewater sports destination in the peninsula. Different stretches of the river and its tributaries are used for various activities such as kayaking, canoeing, rafting and tubing. The

---

DISTANCE 72km (45 miles) north of KL; the tour itself covers 8km (5 miles)
TIME A full day
START Kuala Kubu Bharu
END Chiling Waterfall
POINTS TO NOTE

Take the half-hourly Mega Kota bus no. 66 (1½ hours) or the KTM Komuter to Rawang and catch the local bus (1 hour) or taxi (½ hour) to KKB. An inter-state taxi from Pudu-raya (75 minutes) costs RM200 one way. There is no accommodation in KKB, so make this a day trip or combine it with tour 11 (Fraser's Hill).

Food and Drink
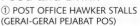

① POST OFFICE HAWKER STALLS (GERAI-GERAI PEJABAT POS)
Jalan Abdul Hamid, opposite the post office; daily 6am–2pm; $
This row of 10 hawker stalls offer simple Malay and Chinese food. Try the wild-boar curry from stall no. 7 and steamed Chinese buns from stall no. 8.

② RESTORAN NINETY EIGHT
33 & 34 Jalan Dato' Balai; tel: 03-6064 1189; Tue–Sun 4pm–midnight. $
Cantonese fare such as wild-boar curry and the Hakka speciality of *khaw yoke*, thick slices of pork belly with yam.

③ KEDAI MAKANAN GOVINDAMAH
9 Jalan Abdul Hamid; tel: 03-6064 5723; daily 7am–1am; $
Home-cooked spicy South Indian meals and breads.

Above from left:
Orang Asli kids
making a splash;
Sungai Chiling.

Dam History
Sungai Selangor
had been dammed
before, in 1883 and
1926. Both times the
river broke its banks,
flooding the original
town of Kuala Kubu,
which used to be
further downstream
from the current
town's location.
The Temuan believe
the river is haunted
by a red dragon
spirit that caused
the dam to burst
its banks twice.

Below right:
Kampung Gerachi
Jaya, an Orang
Asli settlement.

latter involves floating down the river in a rubber tube; it is impossible to control but a lot of fun. Unless you have your own watersports gear, it is best to join a tour organised by an adventure tour company. A number of them, based in KL or KKB, offer half- and full-day whitewater sports tours with instruction *(see p.71)*. Note that basic certification in whitewater kayaking requires a minimum of three days. You can also combine your tour with a rainforest trek.

To get to the starting points of the whitewater action, use the road leading to Fraser's Hill. Part of this road skirts the **Sungai Selangor Dam**, which supplies water to parts of Selangor and KL. Along the way, there are pleasant vistas of this blue expanse of water and the surrounding 600-ha (1,480-acre) forested area.

KAMPUNG GERACHI JAYA

Some of the best views are from **Kampung Gerachi Jaya ❷**, atop a steep hill

about 4km (2 miles) from KKB. This is the village of one of two indigenous Orang Asli communities that were affected by the construction of the dam. Despite widespread protests against the drowning of their ancestral lands and the destruction of traditional liveli-hoods, the Orang Asli, who are from the Temuan group, were relocated. Their new contemporary-style settle-ments, however, are dissonant with the reality of their largely forest-bound lives.

Always ask the Tok Batin, the village head, for permission to walk around in the village, and do bring gifts of rice, biscuits or tea or coffee. The Temuan speak little English and are very shy but are open to visits by tourists. You might catch a glimpse of traditional activities like blowpipe making or basket weaving. Some handicraft might be available for sale.

In these modern times, about half the Temuan earn an income through the collection and sale of jungle pro-duce like bamboo and fruit to the townsfolk. Others work in rubber and

oil palm estates and have odd jobs in town. Whitewater sports and nature tourism have also given them a few new skills and income opportunities.

Dam Information Centre

Back on the main road, the next stop is the **Dam Information Centre** ❸ (Tue–Sun 9am–4pm), which has an exhibition on the dam project. This is also where you can view the dam's 30m/yd-wide spillway, into which water overflows during the wet season.

KAMPUNG PERTAK

Driving on for another 3km (2 miles), you come to the other new Temuan settlement, **Kampung Pertak** ❹. The houses are spread along the banks of Sungai Luit, a beautiful stream that tumbles over boulders large and small. Drive to the end of the village and walk down to the stream. If you are not up for any strenuous activity, this is the perfect place to sunbathe, picnic and splash around in. Again, if you want to visit the village, do ask for permission.

CHILING WATERFALL

A popular starting point for white-water sports is a five-minute drive from Kampung Pertak, at an old metal bridge known locally as the **Rainbow Bridge** because of its arched shape. Adventure sports operators sometimes use this bridge for abseiling activities. On the right side of the road is a trail that leads to the lovely three-tier **Chiling Waterfall** ❺. The 1½-hour

trek follows the swift Sungai Chiling, a tributary of Sungai Selangor, and involves six river crossings (so do not attempt this trek yourself). The rewards of a picnic on the rocks and a swim in the clear waters of the waterfall are well worth the journey. The picnic spot is by the bottom-most tier of the Chiling Waterfall, which gushes 20m (66ft) into a very deep pool. It is best not to do this trek after rain, as the canyon is prone to flash floods.

Dipterocarp Forest

The forest here is mainly lowland dipterocarp forest, characterised by gigantic trees and herbaceous species such as ferns and gingers. The vegetation fringing the river comprises species that grow well in open areas with strong sunlight, such as creepers, ferns, shrubs and semi-aquatic plants. These riverine areas are important corridors for birds and other animals.

Whitewater Sports Operators

Recommended adventure sports operators include: Box Tracks Adventure (tel: 019-344 3214, 03-6065 1767; www. tracksadventures. com.my); Pierose Swiftwater (tel: 013-361 3991, 03-6064 5040; www.raft malaysia.com); Khersonese Eco-X (tel: 016-690 2425, 03-7722 3511; www. thepaddlerz.com); and Endemicguides (tel: 016-383 2222, 03-5512 3012; www. endemicguides.com).

Below: abseiling off the Rainbow Bridge.

FRASER'S HILL

Enjoy highland weather and breathtaking views on this hill resort, which sits 1,500m (4,900ft) above sea level. Weekenders come here to unwind, explore jungle trails and tee off at the picturesque golf course.

DISTANCE 104km (65 miles) north of KL; trails cover varying distances
TIME A full day, or overnight
START/END Information Centre
POINTS TO NOTE

It takes around two hours to get to Fraser's Hill from KL by car or taxi. An inter-state taxi costs about RM200. Alternatively, get to Kuala Kubu Bharu *(see p.69)* in time to catch the only bus to Fraser's at 10.30am, or take the KTM Komuter to Rawang and take a taxi from there to Fraser's (RM50).

British Malaya's first hill station, **Fraser's Hill**, attracts weekenders from KL with its cool weather (daytime temperature averages 20°C/68°F), misty, forested landscapes and serene atmosphere. It is great for an escape from the lowland heat, but note that food, activities and accommodation are limited. The jump-off point for the hill resort is Kuala Kubu Bharu (KKB; *see p.69*).

ROUTE 55

The road from KKB to Fraser's Hill is a scenic, thickly forested one that winds uphill. It is part of the historic first path built across the Titiwangsa

Winding Roads
Route 55 and the roads up and down Fraser's Hill are winding with sharp curves. Travellers who are prone to car-sickness should be prepared. Try not to drive on these roads at night as the mist can be thick.

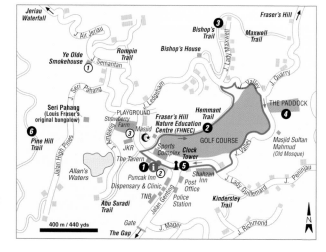

Range, which is known as **Route 55** today. In the late 19th century, gold was transported by mule along this road from Raub, the El Dorado of the peninsula then, located on the east of the mountains, to Port Klang on the west coast via the old town of Kuala Kubu. One of the many who cashed in on the transport and supply provisioning on this road was the accountant-turned-mule-transport-entrepreneur Louis James Fraser. He ran a gambling and opium den for miners and planters as well. The hill was named after him, although he had long disappeared by the time the hill station was built in 1910.

Route 55 climbs up a slope. As you ascend, note the change in vegetation. Trees much shorter than the giants of the lowlands are common at these higher altitudes. At 1,200m (3,940ft), you will see more conifers and tree ferns.

The Gap

At the base of Fraser's Hill, there are two turn-offs. The first is at **The Gap**, which is historically the gap between the boundaries of the states of Selangor and Pahang. (Fraser's Hill is actually part of Pahang.) It was also the mid-point on the mule-and-bullock-cart transport route during Louis Fraser's time. A colonial resthouse here hints of the architecture you will see at the top of the hill, but it is badly maintained. The Gap used to be the sole pathway to and from the resort, but today, it is used only by descending vehicles. Ascending vehicles now take another, newer, road further on.

COLONIAL BUNGALOWS

The resort is scattered over seven hills, on which sit a series of English grey-stone bungalows surrounded by neat English gardens blooming with roses and hollyhocks. The tiny town centre around the clock tower, however, has some disastrous newer additions, while the modern high-rise hotels in the area also fail to blend with the landscape.

The Smokehouse

Of note is the **Smokehouse Hotel and Restaurant** (tel: 09-362 2226; www. thesmokehouse.com.my/fh), a Tudor-style concern built in 1924, complete with overstuffed chintz covered sofas and a fireplace. Even if you do not stay here, you must not pass up tea and warm scones in its lovely garden (daily 3–6pm). The restaurant also serves the best dinner in Fraser's Hill, see ⑪①.

WALKS

Because of its proximity to KL, Fraser's Hill is crowded at weekends, but there are enough walks and trails to take you away from the madding crowd.

Food and Drink 🍴

① SMOKEHOUSE HOTEL AND RESTAURANT

Jalan Jeriau; tel: 09-362 2226; daily dinner 6.30–9.30pm; $$$$

This does a good job with traditional English fare such as pot roast and Yorkshire pudding. Classical music and a log fire add to the atmosphere. A dress code applies for dinner.

Above from far left: well-traversed path on the Bishop's Trail; conifer forest bordering Fraser's Hill; giant fern in the twilight; old bungalows stand amid rolling hills.

Above: tea at the Smokehouse.

What's in a Name
The retreat's first four colonial bungalows were named after famous World War I gun shelters because limited funds allowed only tiny buildings to be erected. Later buildings were named after Pahang's British Residents or their wives; these have been renamed after places in Pahang.

Guided Walks
Guided nature walks
are great if you have
had little exposure to a
highland rainforest or
are an inexperienced
trekker. Birdwatching
and night trekking
tours are also
available. Call Durai
(mobile tel: 013-983
1633) or check with
your hotel.

Below: epiphyte-
clad tree in Fraser's
montane forest.

Jeriau Waterfall

From the Smokehouse Hotel, turn left
and follow the road for about 4km (2
miles) to **Jeriau Waterfall**. Although
this 10-m (30-ft) high waterfall is not
quite spectacular, it is refreshing and
a good location for birdwatching. Note
that the steps leading to the waterfall
are slippery after rain.

Golf Course

The ring road around the golf course
makes for a pleasant two-hour walk, and
brings you past the old bungalows and
newer resorts. The picturesque nine-
hole golf course is very old. It was carved
out of an old tin mine, and is one of the
few public courses in the country. You
can rent golf sets and other accessories
(tel: 09-362 2129; daily 8am–7pm).

JUNGLE TRAILS

There are also eight jungle trails of
varying lengths, all well-marked and
easy to follow, with most being quite

easy-going. For these trails, make sure
you are wearing sturdy shoes and
check trail conditions and get a map at
the **Information Centre ❶** (tel: 09-
362 2201; Sun–Fri 8am–9pm, Sat
9am–10pm) in the town centre.

Hemmant Trail

This is a longish route that takes in
both the ring road and a short forest
trail. Start at the Information Centre.
Turn left onto Jalan Genting and walk
uphill for about 200m/yd till you see
the sign for the **Fraser's Hill Nature
Education Centre** on your right. Turn
onto the road and this brings you to
the **Hemmant Trail ❷**, which mean-
ders for 2½km (1½ miles) through the
forest before reaching the ring road
again. Skirting the golf course, the trail
(named after the architect of the
course) leads you through the moist,
mossy forest that defines the highland
environment. Along the way, keep an
eye out for monkeys, squirrels, beetles
and trapdoor spiders.

Bishop's Trail

When you reach the paved road, you
have two choices. If you are game for
another forest trail, turn left and walk
along the road till you come to the
Bishop's Trail ❸, named after the
clergyman who, in 1910, went looking
for the missing Louis Fraser but failed
to find him, and ended up establishing
this hill retreat. This short trail has
been turned into an interesting interpretive trail, complete with distance
markers, informative signboards and
learning stations.

Otherwise, to return to the town centre, turn right at the end of the Hemmant Trail where the paved road loops back to your starting point. The road skirts the golf course for most of the remaining 3km (1½ miles). You pass a **paddock** ❹, where you can ride a horse or try archery. Continue on this road till you reach the **town centre** ❺. The famous clock tower is actually a later mock-Tudor addition to the cluster of original colonial buildings, which comprise the post office, police station and medical dispensary.

Pine Hill Trail

If you are fit, you may wish to consider taking on the most challenging of the trails – the steep, guided-only 6-km (4-mile) **Pine Hill Trail** ❻, which goes up to 1,450m (4,750ft) and rewards with breathtaking views. The trail takes you through montane habitats with vegetation and wildlife found above heights of 1,500m (4,900ft). As you ascend higher, you see the vegetation change. At the lower altitudes, the montane forest features trees with buttresses and epiphytes such as orchids, while the upper montane forest in the higher elevations are home to shorter trees and more shrubs, with thicker leaves.

BIRDWATCHING

The forests of Fraser's Hill have some of the richest birdlife in the peninsula. While on the trails, you may chance to bump into groups standing rock-still and peering intently through binocu-

lars. There are an estimated 275 local and migratory species and this has put Fraser's Hill on the birdwatching map. During the annual International Bird Race (www.pkbf.org.my/events.htm), usually held in the middle of the year and co-organised by the Malaysian Nature Society, WWF Malaysia and the Fraser's Hill Development Corporation, international teams of birders race to identify the largest number of bird species on the official checklist.

Dining Options

There are a couple of grocery shops (daily 9am–10pm) in the town centre where you can buy snacks, bottled water and bread. For more substantial meals, try **Restoran Hill View**, see ⑪②, for Chinese food, or **Mimi Taman Strawberi dan Kafe**, see ⑪③, for Malay and café-style food.

Food and Drink 🍴

② RESTORAN HILL VIEW

Puncak Inn; tel: 09-362 2231; daily 10am–9pm; $
Operated by a local family who have been residents on the hill for two generations, this serves Chinese meals and decent pub grub. The chicken and lamb chops are recommended.

③ MIMI TAMAN STRAWBERI DAN KAFE

Jalan Genting, opposite the mosque; daily 9am–5pm; $
At this little café next to strawberry and tomato patches, you can sip hot strawberry tea or slurp ice-cold juice. Waffles, chicken rice and assorted Malay dishes are available.

Above from far left: forest trail; Jeriau Waterfall; the town centre with its clock tower; hikers and bird-watchers.

Self-Drive Tours

If you have your own transport, note that there are a number of good drives around the area, such as the Jalan Peninjau loop that goes past the holiday bungalows of multinational corporations. The roads are winding, however, so be careful when driving.

GENTING HIGHLANDS

Perched on the Titiwangsa Range 1,870m (6,120ft) above sea level, Genting Highlands is Malaysia's Las Vegas. The kitschy resort draws families, gamblers and day-trippers looking for respite from the lowland heat.

DISTANCE Genting Highlands is 51km (31¾ miles) northeast of KL

TIME A full day, or overnight

START Skyway station

END Chin Swee Caves Temple

POINTS TO NOTE

Take a bus (1 hour) from the Puduraya Bus Station or KL Sentral; the fare is inclusive of the Skyway ride. Taxis to Genting Highlands (tel: 03-2078 5353; RM60–70 one way) also depart from Puduraya and are able to pick you up from your hotel in KL. The Genting Highlands Resort also offers packages that include room and transport. The daytime temperature hovers around 18–23°C (67–72°F).

Accommodation

Genting Highlands is visited by 18 million tourists a year, so it gets pretty crowded. Book your accommodation at the Genting Highlands Resort (tel: 03-2718 1118; www.genting.com.my) beforehand. The resort comprises six hotels and apartments *(see p.115)*.

The start of your Genting experience is the spectacular 24-hour **Skyway** ❶ cable-car ride. Gliding above a blanket of montane vegetation, the ride is said to be the world's fastest, covering the 3.4-km (2-mile) journey in 11 minutes.

INDOOR THEME PARK

The ride ends at the Genting Hotel. Follow the signs to the **Genting Indoor Theme Park** ❷ (Mon–Fri 9am–midnight, Sat 8am–1am, Sun 8am–midnight; charge). Arcade games and children's rides are the main attractions.

CASINO

Follow the signs again to the escalator that goes up to the Genting Hotel

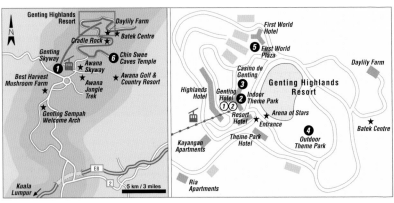

lobby. Take the lift there to the **Casino de Genting ❸** (daily 24 hours; minimum age 21), on the first floor, for table games, slots and keno, spread over 18,600sq m (200,000sq ft). You need to be appropriately dressed to enter. The dress code is long trousers and collared shirt or t-shirt, or the traditional Malaysian batik shirt for men. Sandals and caps are not allowed; neither are mobile phones nor cameras. Muslims are forbidden to enter.

OUTDOOR THEME PARK

Return to the lobby, turn left and follow directions to the **Genting Outdoor Theme Park ❹** (Mon 9am–7pm, Tue–Fri 10am–7pm, Sat 8am–10pm, Sun 8am–8pm; standard charge covers limited rides). Set around an artificial lake are numerous rides, including the double-loop Corkscrew roller coaster and the hand-gliding Flying Coaster (separate charge).

FIRST WORLD PLAZA

Over at the **First World Plaza ❺** is the **First World Plaza Indoor Theme Park** (Mon–Fri 9am–midnight, Sat 8am–1am, Sun 8am–midnight; charge), with signature attractions such as the 4D Motion Master Theatre (separate charge), a 4D movie experience, and the Genting Sky Venture, a wind tunnel for skydiving (separate charge).

There are 90-odd eateries in the resort to choose from, including food courts, fast-food outlets and fancy **restaurants**, see 🍴① and 🍴②.

CHIN SWEE TEMPLE

For some quiet, take the free shuttle from the resort to the **Chin Swee Caves Temple ❻** (daily 9am–11pm). Perched on a steep slope, the temple honours the reverend Chin Swee, who purportedly inspired Lim Goh Tong, Genting's founder, to build the resort. Carvings on the outside walls depict Chin Swee's life and his statue sits in the main chamber. To the left of the main temple is a nine-storey pagoda with Buddha statues; climb to the top for great views. The best view, though, is from the **Sky Terrace**, which overlooks the mountain. A path winds from here up to the graphic **Ten Chambers of Hell**.

ENTERTAINMENT

If it is evening, return to the resort for a meal and a show. Three theatres feature entertainment such as cabaret dinner shows, musicals and concerts.

Food and Drink 🍴

① SPICE GARDEN

Lobby Floor, Genting Hotel; tel: 03-6101 1118; daily noon–midnight; $$
Spice Garden serves well-prepared North Indian and Middle Eastern dishes. Try the tandoori prawns and mutton *roghan josh*.

② THE OLIVE

Lobby Floor, Genting Hotel; tel: 03-6101 1118; daily noon–2.30pm and 6–10.30pm; $$$
This classy dining room serves Continental cuisine with contemporary twists. Succulent Wagyu beef is the house speciality.

Above from far left: cable-car ride up to Genting Highlands; inside the Genting complex.

Theme Park Pass
You can buy a pass to individual theme parks or one to all theme parks.

Rags to Riches
Genting's founder, the late Lim Goh Tong, left his village in China for Malaya at the age of 20, a pauper, and slowly learned the ropes in the construction industry. In the 1960s, while on a job in the hill station, Cameron Highlands, he hit upon the idea of building a hill resort close to KL. With support from the first prime minister, he worked against scepticism and a forbidding terrain to build what is today a darling of corporate Malaysia, a US$8.9 billion conglomerate with tens of thousands of employees.

KUALA GANDAH

Visit a forest recreational park before seeing Asian elephants up close at the Kuala Gandah National Elephant Conservation Centre. Nearby is Kampung Kuala Ganlah, home to the Che' Wong indigenous community.

DISTANCE Kuala Gandah is 120km (75 miles) northeast of KL

TIME A full day

START Hutan Lipur Lentang

END Kuala Gandah National Elephant Conservation Centre

POINTS TO NOTE

Hire a car or taxi from the Puduraya Outstation Taxi (tel: 03-2078 3525; RM250 for a round trip). Take the Karak Highway towards Kuantan; have change ready to pay tolls.

Budget four hours for the other attractions so you can reach Kuala Gandah for the 1pm programme. Bring a change of clothes if you intend to get into the river with the elephants.

The **Karak Highway** is a beautiful road that snakes up the Titiwangsa Range, making for a nice drive. As you climb, breathtaking scenery unfolds – dramatic mountains clothed in lush tree cover are set off by azure skies.

HUTAN LIPUR LENTANG

From the Gombak toll, drive for about 30km (18½ miles) till you see an exit on your left at KM 48 signposted **Hutan Lipur Lentang ❶** (Lentang Forest Recreational Park). Turn off here, drive under the highway, turning left again to get to the park. On the right is the office of the Forestry Department (tel: 09-2330 484; Mon–Fri 8am–5pm, Sat–Sun 10am–5pm),

Che' Wong

Like many indigenous communities, the Che' Wong are transitioning to a moneyed economy. If you buy their products, the money goes directly to the handicraft producers. You can also make a donation into a box in their village; this is distributed among the community.

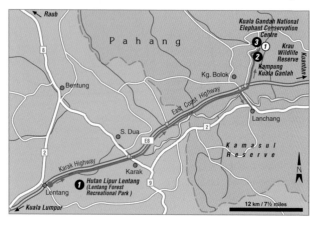

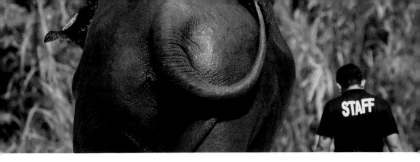

which manages the park. This is a lovely spot to take a break. Pack food from the city or from the canteen (8am–5pm) and picnic under the shady trees along the cold, swift stream. You can also trek along the river, but will need to register with the Forestry Department, as the river level can rise suddenly after rain. Note that the park gets very crowded at weekends and on public holidays.

KAMPUNG KUALA GANLAH

Get back onto the Karak Highway and drive for another 50km (31 miles) before exiting at Lanchang. After 13km (8 miles), you reach a village of stilted houses. This is **Kampung Kuala Ganlah ❷**, home to the Che' Wong, an Orang Asli indigenous group who reside in Central Pahang. Right by the road is a large triangular hut housing a handicraft centre (daily 10am–1pm), where you can buy baskets and bangles woven by the women. This initiative was spearheaded by a Malay officer of the Department of Islamic Development (Jakim) to help some 20–30 women of the 150-member community earn income. The Che' Wong are largely dependent on the forest for their livelihood, although many men now have jobs in plantations and factories. Take a look around their village. The houses are fine examples of Che' Wong traditional architecture, with walls of bark and finely woven thatches. Do respect that these are homes and ask for permission if you want to take photographs.

KUALA GANDAH ELEPHANT CENTRE

Down the road is the **Kuala Gandah National Elephant Conservation Centre ❸** (tel: 09-2790 391; Sun–Thur 8am–4.45pm, Fri 8am–12.30pm and 2.45–5pm; donation). Have lunch at **Saudi Café**, see ⑪①, and browse the interpretation centre before the 1pm programme, which begins with a video. The centre's six elephants have been trained to interact with people. You then get to feed, ride and bathe the Asian elephants under the wildlife officers' supervision. Rides are limited to 120 people per day.

The activities help raise awareness of the centre's purpose as a temporary base for elephants that are being relocated from one place to another. When their natural forest habitats are taken over by agriculture, the elephants are forced to feed on cultivated land, and are then chased away by planters. Elephants that cannot keep up with their herds are abandoned. Older elephants are relocated to state and national parks, but unfortunately babies almost never adapt again to the wild and are sent to zoos. Four babies are being cared for at the centre; they are occasionally brought out to be habituated to humans.

Above from far left: a trainer and his ward; rear view.

Lokimala
The grand old lady you will encounter at the elephant conservation centre is Lokimala, a 70-year-old from India that understands only the Assamese language. She is trained to shepherd wild elephants as they are being relocated.

Food and Drink ⑪
① SAUDI CAFÉ
Kuala Gandah Elephant Centre; daily 6am–3pm; $
Simple Malay meals. Order the fried chicken to go with the tasty *nasi goreng kampung* (fried rice).

Endangered Species
Only 800–1,000 elephants remain in the wilds of Malaysia.

KUALA SELANGOR

Defined by its coastal location, Kuala Selangor charms with its historical sights and unique mangrove ecosystem, birdwatching opportunities, fresh seafood and a riverside that is ablaze with fireflies at night.

DISTANCE Kuala Selangor is 67km (42 miles) northwest of KL; the tour itself covers 16km (9½ miles)
TIME A full day, or overnight
START Bukit Melawati
END Kampung Kuantan
POINTS TO NOTE
Hire a car or taxi to get to Kuala Selangor. Head north on the North-South Expressway, exit at Sungai Buloh and follow the road for 45 minutes till you reach the Assam Jawa junction, where you turn right. Drive for about 10 minutes until you reach Bukit Melawati and the old Kuala Selangor town centre. A taxi from Puduraya (1 hour) costs RM50–60 one way, plus RM20–25 for waiting time. Unless you want to spend more time at the Nature Park, get to Bukit Melawati by the early afternoon and time to end the excursion with the night-time firefly tour.

Weekend Tram
A tram goes around Bukit Melawati on weekends and public holidays 8am–6pm (charge). You can get off and on again at several stops.

Standing at the estuary of the Selangor River, Kuala Selangor was once the capital of the Sultanate of Selangor. The river was a vital means of communication to the otherwise impenetrable interior. It was also the key to political and economic power: those who controlled communications along the river also controlled the hinterland. The state of Selangor had three great river systems – the Langat, Klang and Selangor – and the respective nobilities who controlled these rivers fought constantly for dominance. Ultimately, the group that controlled the Klang became the strongest. Today, the Klang Valley is the nation's fastest-growing urban area, while both Kuala Langat and Kuala Selangor have slipped into obscurity.

BUKIT MELAWATI

Whatever greatness the town of Kuala Selangor once enjoyed remains in the form of an old fort, a lighthouse and a mausoleum on **Bukit Melawati** ❶. The historic hill is located in the old town and directions to it are well signposted. The 1½-km (¾-mile) road around the hill, with huge century-old raintrees and nice lookouts of the surroundings, makes for a pleasant walk. Keep left every time you come to a fork.

Historical Remnants

The second sultan of Selangor built a fort on Bukit Melawati to repel attacks from the Dutch during his reign (1778–1826). The Dutch captured the fort briefly but thereafter many bloody battles were fought over it. As you

walk up the hill, you first pass a **poison well**, once filled with a poisonous mixture of latex and juice from bamboo shoots for torturing traitors. Further along on your right is the Dutch-built **Altingsburg Lighthouse** (closed to the public), opposite of which is a **lookout** with views of the Kuala Selangor Nature Park. Peering over the lookout are six **canons** from the Selangor-Dutch war. The **watchtower** here is where Muslim religious authorities today sight the new moon for key dates in the Muslim calendar, such as the beginning and end of Ramadan, the fasting month. Walk on and you come to the remains of the **Melawati Gate**, the former gateway to the fort.

The last attraction is the **Royal Burial Ground** of the first three sultans of Selangor and their families. Entry to the mausoleum is restricted, but if you peer through the gates, you can see the **Penggawa**, the sacred canon draped with yellow cloth and the sultans' most trusted protector.

Return to the Melawati Gate and descend by the steps down to the foot of the hill. Dubbed **The Hundred Steps**, these were once the only pathway to Kuala Selangor town from the dock below. The dock area is now the Kuala Selangor Nature Park. Turn right and walk through the housing estate to reach the park entrance.

KUALA SELANGOR NATURE PARK

The **Kuala Selangor Nature Park ②** (Taman Alam Kuala Selangor) holds over 324ha (800 acres) of an important river ecosystem that includes a vital crop of mangroves. A nominal entry

Above from far left: Dutch cannons on Bukit Melawati; Altingsburg Lighthouse; mudskipper; exploring the mudflats from a boardwalk.

Canon Protector
Discovered in 1966 in Sungai Buloh, 19km (12 miles) from Kuala Selangor, the Penggawa was first brought to Jugra, Selangor's second capital. It was said that the canon 'refused' to stay put and was finally brought to its current location to guard the old sultans.

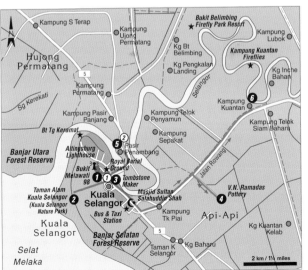

Above: a mangrove seedling and the exposed stilt roots of a mangrove plant.

Above from left:
birders in action; male fiddler crab; seafood at Pasir Penambang; crafting Indian pottery.

Breeding Season
The beginning of the year is the breeding season of grey herons. This is a great time to watch mating behaviour, which includes elaborate neck movements. The birds become very noisy and their beaks and legs also turn from yellow to deep orange.

Pottery Purchases
V.N. Ramadas Pottery also makes clay items that you can buy. These include Indian pots that are used for cooking curry – the clay is said to enhance the taste of the food. You can also buy little oil lamps and figurines of Indian deities.

fee helps the Malaysian Nature Society (MNS) maintain the park. Register at the **Visitors' Centre** (tel: 03-3289 2294; daily 8am–6pm; charge). The centre has comprehensive information and nature-themed souvenirs for sale. Simple chalets and dormitories are available for overnight stays *(see p.115)*.

Birdwatching

Migratory waterbirds are the main attraction here. The best season to see them is from September to April when they stop over on their way to Australia to escape the northern winter. Before your walk, get a copy of the birding guide from the Visitors' Centre. There are several hides around the park for birdwatching. At the end of the **Egret Trail** is a 10-m (30-ft) watchtower, from where you can check out the brackish lake; hundreds of grey herons and purple herons congregate and breed at the lake.

Trails

Three trails of lengths varying from 300m/yd to 2km (1½ miles) wind through mangrove and secondary forests and the lake system. Boardwalks provide access to the mudflats and extend to the river mouth. Try spotting Silver Leaf Monkeys, common Long-tailed Macaques and even otters. The mudflats are a good place to see crabs, mudskippers and waders. First-time visitors to a mangrove should take the informative hour-long guided tour (book one week ahead; charge). The trails are not shaded, so bring a hat, sunblock and plenty of water, and apply insect repellent liberally.

TRADITIONAL CRAFT

Walk back to town for tea at the **Restoran Waterfall Café**, see ⑪①. Across the main road is a hillock dotted with rocks. Cross the busy road carefully and turn right, walking along the foot of the hill till you come to a little shed beneath a tree.

Tombstone Maker

The shed is the workshop of Casey the **tombstone maker ❸**, who laboriously crafts Muslim tombstones from granite. What makes him even more interesting is that he is ethnically Chinese and a Taoist, but has learnt the Jawi script in order to carve the Quranic verses on the tombstones. His clients come from all over the country and include royalty. He also makes traditional pestles and mortars as well as grinding stones, which are essential items at traditional Hindu weddings.

Food and Drink 🍴

① RESTORAN WATERFALL CAFÉ
88 Jalan Stesen, Kuala Selangor;
tel: 03-3289 2388; daily
10am–8.45pm; $
A family-owned café offering simple fare including sandwiches, pasta and Chinese seafood dishes.

② RIVER VIEW SEAFOOD RESTAURANT
1 Jalan Besar, Pasir Penambang; tel: 03-3289 2238; daily 11am–10pm; $
Offers excellent views and tasty Chinese seafood meals. The fresh fish comes in variations such as steamed, black pepper, and sweet and sour.

V.N. Ramadas Pottery

You need your own wheels to get to your next stop. Head back towards the Assam Jawa turnoff, where you turn left onto Jalan Rawang. Drive for 8km (5 miles) till you come to Jalan Keretapi Lama. Turn right onto this road and about 1km (½ mile) further is **V.N. Ramadas Pottery** ❹ (tel: 03-3289 1054; by appointment only; free) on your right. This is the largest and most established of this area's seven traditional Indian pottery makers. Watch potters fashion their trademark round-bottom pots called *mann panai* using a modified potter's wheel with the quirky name *pugmillm jolly jongels*. The earthern pots are then fired in a brick kiln and sun-dried. The pots are used to cook a traditional rice and milk dish during Ponggal, the Tamil thanksgiving festival.

PASIR PENAMBANG

For dinner, head for the Chinese fishing village of **Pasir Penambang** ❺. Get onto the main road again, driving towards Bukit Melawati. Cross the bridge and a turn-off on the left takes you past wooden houses on stilts to the village centre. In the daytime, this is a bustling wholesale and retail seafood centre. The main street is lined with eateries and shops selling seafood of all manner, from anchovy-based condiments to prawn snacks. Drop by the seafood-processing warehouses before you settle down to a seafood meal with views of the river at the breezy **River View Seafood Restaurant**, see ⑪②.

KAMPUNG KUANTAN

After dinner, drive on to **Kampung Kuantan** ❻, using Jalan Rawang. From the turn-off, continue for 9km (5½ miles) to the firefly tour jetty (daily 8–10.30pm, ticket office opens from 7pm). Local boatmen take you out on a 40-minute ride on the river (four persons at RM40 per boat), passing through *berembang* mangroves, whose drooping branches are the habitat for millions of tiny male fireflies flashing synchronously in the dark. Said to be the world's brightest fireflies, these flash at a rate of three flashes per second. Avoid rainy nights, as there will be fewer fireflies to behold.

Firefly Tours

The Kampung Kuantan boatmen who operate the firefly tours are all locals and use wooden paddle boats to ferry tourists. Tours are also offered by a large operator at Kampung Belimbing north of Kampung Kuantan, but it uses large boats, whose wake is said to erode the riverbanks. These tours are also less personal.

The Mangrove World

As the tides rise and fall, mangrove forests become wet, then dry, several times a day. In this harsh environment, mangroves have adapted in unique ways. For example, excessive salt is filtered out at the root level or sweated out through the leaves. Mangrove leaves also have a waxy top with fine hair and scales on the bottom to prevent water loss. Some seeds have a tough coat to withstand saltwater until they are carried to a suitable place to grow; others are designed to float with the tide. Mangroves' extensive root systems are also a natural barrier against coastal erosion: the roots make excellent silt traps, which raise the banks and actually help to 'reclaim' land. Rotting leaves and debris are food for crabs, snails and mudskippers, which are food for fish, prawns and shellfish. These, in turn, support different types of birds and mammals, and humans.

PETALING JAYA

Located southwest of KL, Petaling Jaya is typified by sprawling housing estates and small town centres, but it also boasts an excellent museum and conservatory, and a thrilling water theme park.

DISTANCE Petaling Jaya is 20km (13 miles) southwest of KL; the tour itself covers 15km (9¼ miles)
TIME A full day
START Wat Chetawan
END Sunway City
POINTS TO NOTE
Take the LRT to Taman Jaya and hire a taxi for half a day. You can walk the 1½km (¾ miles) to the first stop, but will still need to hire a taxi from there on. If you forgo Sunway City, complete the first half of the tour in the morning and continue with tour 16 (Klang), 17 (Pulau Carey) or 18 (Putrajaya).

Thai Festivals
Wat Chetawan is most colourful during Thai festivals like the Songkran water festival (mid April), the full-moon celebration Loy Krathong (12th full moon of the year), as well as the Buddha's birthday, Wesak Day (May).

Ancient Cloths
The Museum of Asian Art also has a fine textile collection, which features the ancient *patola* cloth *(above)*, a precious regional trading commodity in the 15th and 16th centuries.

Petaling Jaya offers a look at suburban Malaysia. Originally developed as a low-cost housing scheme in the late 1950s, PJ is today a middle-class city, home to half a million people.

WAT CHETAWAN

Glinting roofs welcome you to the Siamese temple complex, **Wat Cheta-wan ❶** (Jalan Pantai 9/7; tel: 03-7956 2791; daily 7am–9.30pm). One of the few royal-sponsored temples outside Thailand, this is a religious community centre for Malaysian Thais, although its devotees also include non-Thais.

Architecturally, the *wat* (or temple) is impressive. Of note are its steep multi-tiered orange-tiled roofs, whose ends are decorated with curling ends called *chofah*. The buildings also feature intricate carvings, miniature glass tiles and the liberal use of gold. The main prayer hall houses several Buddha images. Open-sided pavilions dot the grounds; in one sits a four-faced statue of Buddha that watches over all four corners of the world, while another pavilion hosts Guan Yin, the Goddess of Mercy. A smaller hall pays tribute to Buddhist abbots whose lifelike statues have Malay titles, reflecting their northern peninsular Malaysian and southern Thai origins.

From Wat Chetawan, you can walk or drive to Jalan Chantek for an Indian brunch at **Raju's Restaurant**, see ⑪①, or further up Jalan Gasing to **Satellite Chicken Rice**, see ⑪②, for a heartier meal.

MUSEUM OF ASIAN ART

Move on to Universiti Malaya, the country's first university, to visit two attractions. The **Museum of Asian Art ❷** (Muzium Seni Asia; tel: 03-7967 3805; Mon–Fri 9am–5pm, except Fri 12.15–2.45pm; free; book ahead for a guided tour) is a gem show-

casing 6,000 pieces of art – mainly ceramics – spanning 4,000 years of Malaysian and Asian history. The museum's *kendi* (a water container with a spout and no handles) collection is the world's largest public collection of its kind, covering 1,000 years and representing different countries in East and Southeast Asia. The container's shapes and designs are clues to fascinating cultural and social practices and trade patterns of the region. Interestingly, although the container was used extensively in the peninsula, it was never manufactured locally but sourced from neighbouring countries.

Chancellory

Take Lingkungan Budi to your next stop, passing the home of the university's chancellor, the **Dewan Tunku Canselor**, on your right. This building is influenced by the style of the 1950s architect Le Corbusier, and is typical of the era when functionality, instead of indigenous design, reigned over Malaysia's institutional buildings.

RIMBA ILMU

About 1km (½ mile) from the chancellory, turn left onto Ambang Asuhan Jepun. Continue for another 2km (1 mile) before you reach **Rimba Ilmu ❸** (tel: 03-7967 4685/6; rimba.um.edu. my; Mon–Thur 9am–1pm and 2–4pm, Fri 9am–noon and 2.45–4pm; charge), or the Forest of Knowledge. This botanical garden is one of the most important biological conservato-

Above from far left: gilded Buddha statues in Wat Chetawan; a *kendi* at the Museum of Asian Art; winged dipterocarp seed on display at Rimba Ilmu's interpretive centre; rainforest trail.

Food and Drink

① RAJU'S RESTAURANT
27 Jalan Chantek 5/13; tel: 03-7956 1361; daily 6.30am–10pm; $
With tables under shady trees, this is a lovely venue for brunch; tuck into rice or breads with various South Indian curries, pickles and crispy *papadom* wafers.

② SATELLITE CHICKEN RICE
103 Jalan Gasing; tel: 03-7956 6830; daily 10am–midnight; $
This long-standing restaurant serves great Hainanese chicken rice – fluffy rice flavoured with chicken stock and accompanied with steamed or roasted chicken; crunchy bean sprouts are a nice side order.

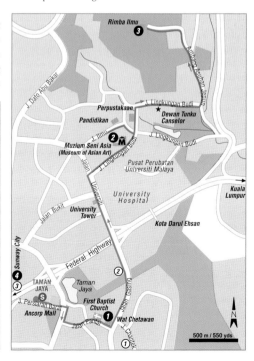

Above from left:
kitsch Sunway
Pyramid mall;
Indian shop selling
flower garlands.

Above: Sunway
Pyramid's indoor
ice-skating rink.

Busy Lagoon

The Sunway Lagoon
(below right) is
busiest at weekends,
in the school holidays
and in December.
Although the park
can accommodate
up to 70,000 visitors
a day, it's a good idea
to avoid it at peak
periods altogether.

G-Force X

A highlight of the
Sunway Lagoon, the
G-Force X is a
reverse bungy where
you are catapulted up
to a height of 65m
(210ft) before a 360-
degree, stomach-
churning turn. It is run
by New Zealand's
A.J. Hackett. The ride
is located within the
Dry Park, so you will
have to pay two
entrance fees.

ries in Malaysia. Begin at its excellent
interpretive exhibition on rainforests
and the environment, then stroll
through **The Garden**, a 45-minute
walk through five collections: medic-
inal plants, palms, citrus and citroids
(lime family), ferns and bamboo.

The guided-tour-only **Conservatory
of Rare Plants and Orchids** houses
1,700 plants that are rare or are
becoming rare due to habitat destruction or overcollection. These include
begonia, orchids and giant 'umbrella
leaf' palms. Book the tour a week ahead.

SUNWAY CITY

From Rimba Ilmu, get onto the Federal Highway and drive towards
Klang. After about 7km (4½ miles),
turn off to **Sunway City** ❹ (www.
sunway.com.my).

Sunway Lagoon

This award-winning development,
built on rehabilitated tin-mining land,
hosts the popular **Sunway Lagoon
Water Theme Park** (tel: 03-5635
8000; Mon, Wed–Fri 11am–6pm,

Sat–Sun 10am–6pm, public and
school holidays daily 10am–6pm;
charge). Fashioned after South Africa's
Sun City, this family-friendly venue
is spread over 32ha (80 acres) and has
three different theme parks and the
world's largest man-made surf beach,
complete with artificial waves.

Sunway Pyramid

The adjoining **Sunway Pyramid** (tel:
03-7494 3000; daily 10am–10pm) is
an Egyptian-themed shopping mall
anchored by a giant lion in a sphinx-
like pose. Besides 700 shops and
eateries, the mall has an indoor ice-
skating rink, a 12-screen cineplex and
48-lane bowling alley. Outdoor cafés
line the front of the mall, serving
everything from American coffee to
sushi and hawker fare.

Sunway Resort Hotel and Spa

Next to the mall is the five-star **Sunway
Resort Hotel and Spa** *(see p.117)*, which
also takes a leaf from Sun City's Palace
of the Lost City but has decor inspired
by Malaysian wildlife. It has a popular
Italian restaurant, **Avanti**, see ③.

Food and Drink 🍴

③ AVANTI
Lobby Level, Sunway Resort Hotel &
Spa, Bandar Sunway; tel: 03-7492
8000; Mon–Sat noon–2.30pm,
Sun–Thur 7–10.30pm, Fri–Sat
7–11.30pm; $$$
A great family restaurant, this
American-Italian outlet offers a
wide choice of wood-fired pizzas,
Sunday buffets and value-for-
money weekday set lunches.

KLANG

Klang Valley's liveliest Indian quarter is in Klang, a royal town that feels like a throwback to a gentler era, with quirky architecture and interesting nooks. Off the coast is one of the country's last traditional fishing villages.

Southwestwards from Petaling Jaya *(see p.84)*, the rest of the Klang Valley conurbation roughly follows the Klang River as it flows towards and decants into the sea at Port Klang, Peninsular Malaysia's main port. In between Petaling Jaya and the sea are the Selangor state capital of Shah Alam, worth a brief stop *(see p.90)*, and the genial former capital of Klang, home to a bustling Little India. Off Port Klang are numerous islands, including Pulau Ketam, which is home to a traditional fishing village that has held its own against modern development.

Klang

Klang, the one-time capital of Selangor, was, in fact, one of several capitals of the state, two others being Kuala Langat and Kuala Selangor *(see p.80)*. In earlier times, the warlords of each capital attempted to establish their hegemony, but the 1867 Selangor Civil War established Klang's dominance and consequently led to its development as a major city, fuelled in the early days by tin, a precious commodity then. Today, Klang continues to wear the badge of royal city but it seems more like an idyllic hamlet compared to its far more developed neighbours, Shah Alam and Petaling Jaya. However, this is part of Klang's charm.

DISTANCE Klang is 32km (20 miles) from KL; the morning tour covers 4km (1½ miles)
TIME A full day
START Masjid Sultan Sulaiman
END Pulau Ketam
POINTS TO NOTE
Take the KTM Komuter to Klang (1 hour). The morning tour is a walking tour, after which you may choose to visit Pulau Ketam or continue with tour 17 (Pulau Carey) or 18 (Putrajaya). Alternatively, combine it with tour 14 (Kuala Selangor) or 15 (Petaling Jaya). To get to the other tours, hire a non-metered taxi from the KTM station; the rate should cover the return trip and the waiting fee of RM20 per hour.

Istana Alam Shah

If you have wheels, drive past the official palace *(below)* of the Sultan of Selangor on Jalan Istana. The sprawling white Istana Alam Shah is where investitures and coronations take place. Royal ceremonies are accompanied by the *nobat*, the royal orchestra, which is considered sacred and is housed in a special building; one such Balai Nobat stands in the grounds. Entry to the palace is not allowed, so just peer through the gates.

Royal Architecture

The blend of architectural styles is a testament to the design legacy of anglophile Sultan Alauddin Sulaiman Shah, and is evident in another mosque and a sprawling palace in Jugra (see p.92).

MASJID SULTAN SULAIMAN

Your first stop, the golden-domed **Masjid Sultan Sulaiman** ❶ (Sultan Sulaiman Mosque; daily 8–11am; free) is about 1km (½ mile) from the Klang KTM Komuter station. To get there, walk or take a taxi down Jalan Raya Timur. Built by the British in 1932 as a gift to Sultan Alauddin Sulaiman Shah, who was also a knight of the British Empire, it has an eclectic blend of neoclassical, Mughal and Arabic architectural styles, complete with colourful stained-glass features. To the left of the mosque is a peaceful royal mausoleum. To enter the buildings, check with the guard first and make sure your arms and legs are covered; women must have their hair covered.

THE OLD STALL

Head back towards the KTM station and walk to Jalan Stesen Satu to **The Old Stall**, see ❶①. Located in a nameless *kopitiam* (coffee shop) within a 1932 shophouse (look up to the pediment to read the date), this eatery is said to be the place where the famous Klang *bak kut teh* originated. This herbal pork soup is synonymous with the town, and is believed to have been brought to the Malay peninsula from Fujian, China, by an immigrant. Now widely available across the country, the dish is available only for breakfast at The Old Stall and is savoured with strong Chinese tea, which you brew yourself. The dining experience is quite interesting, so give it a try.

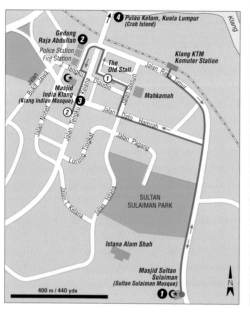

Food and Drink

① THE OLD STALL
Jalan Stesen Satu (next to a car park); daily 5–11am; $
The Old Stall is said to be where the famous Klang *bak kut teh*, a hearty meaty and herbal soup, originated. Various cuts of pork are available. The soup is usually accompanied by rice and Chinese tea.

② SRI BARATHA MATHA VILAS RESTAURANT
34 Jalan Tengku Kelana;
tel: 03-3372 9657;
daily 6.30am–10.30pm $
Prepared using an original house recipe for over 50 years, its signature spicy Indian *mee goreng* fried noodles is served with slices of crispy battered prawn cakes, tofu and egg. Great with a cold, freshly squeezed lime juice.

GEDUNG RAJA ABDULLAH

After your hearty meal, walk towards the flyover and turn right, crossing underneath it to get to Jalan Gedung Raja Abdullah. Straight ahead is the **Gedung Raja Abdullah** ❷, a warehouse-cum-home built in 1856 by Raja Abdullah, one of the two local chieftains who were involved in the Selangor Civil War. This is Klang's last standing historical building related to tin, the lucrative metal that was behind much bloodshed and the subsequent British interference in local affairs. Typifying the traditional Malay architecture of that period, the building served in modern times as a tin museum but has been closed for renovations for many years now.

LITTLE INDIA

From the Gedung Raja Abdullah, walk along Jalan Gedung Raja Abdullah, past the fire station, to get to **Jalan Tengku Kelana** ❸. At the start of this 700-m/yd road, on the right, is **Masjid India Klang** (Klang Indian Mosque), a 1910 mosque built for the Indian Muslim community.

Jalan Tengku Kelana and its vicinity make up the most vibrant Little India in the Klang Valley. From spices to saris and music to *muruku* (deep-fried snacks), the colours, cacophony and aromas of this ethnic enclave assault from all corners.

A good spot for an authentic Indian meal is **Sri Baratha Matha Vilas Restaurant**, see ⑪②, whose speciality is *mee goreng*, a spicy and delightfully sweet fried noodle dish.

Klang Valley residents know Jalan Tengku Kelana is the best place to shop for Indian goods and services, like arranging flights to India, sari tailoring and fortune telling. If you enjoy shopping or taking photographs, you can easily spend a couple of hours here. The atmosphere here during Deepavali, the year-end Hindu Festival of Lights, is electrifying.

PULAU KETAM

Moving on from Little India, you have two choices. You can continue with another tour *(see Points to Note)* or visit **Pulau Ketam** ❹ (Crab Island), an island fishing community located off

Above from left:
Pulau Ketam
back street;
Mah Meri villagers.

the coast. To get there, take the KTM Komuter to Pelabuhan Klang (Port Klang), about 10km (6 miles) to the west of Klang. Walk to the jetty where ferries to Pulau Ketam run every 45 minutes from 8.45am. The last ferry back to the mainland departs at 5.45pm on weekdays and 6pm on weekends. Note that the 30-minute ferry ride can be tedious as it travels through a monotonous landscape of mangroves.

The Blue Mosque

Hewn in the 1970s out of rubber plantations, the Selangor state capital, Shah Alam, 25km (16 miles) west of KL, is one of the country's best planned cities, with boulevards and huge round-abouts. Its only worthwhile attraction is the grand Selangor state mosque, Masjid Sultan Salahuddin Abdul Aziz Shah (tel: 03-5519 9988; Mon–Fri 9am–5pm, except prayer times), also known as the Blue Mosque. Its distinctive blue dome is one of the most prominent structures of the city – in fact, the dome is bigger than that of London's St Paul's Cathedral. The mosque is laid out along the same lines as the Great Mosque of Mecca and is influenced by contemporary Arabic architecture. To tour the interior of the mosque, remove your footwear and ensure you are appropri-ately dressed. Take the KTM Komuter to Batu Tiga and hire a taxi to take you to the Blue Mosque and back to the station.

Around the Village
Change has been slow to arrive in Pulau Ketam. This old Chinese village is surrounded by lush mangroves, the ecosystem that enables its rich fish-eries. Everything on the island revolves around fishing, whether it is catching or rearing fish, or transport and sup-port services. The entire village is built on stilts over mudflats; extensive path-ways and bridges link the different sections. Many of the houses are still made of wood, with family names proudly displayed over the doorways.

As you walk around the village, keep an eye out for Taoist and Buddhist temples and altars. The deities wor-shipped are connected with the ocean and fisheries, alongside the usual gods of prosperity, wisdom and longevity. Look out also for Brahminy kites that swoop down spectacularly to the fish-rich waters.

Pulau Ketam can be crowded at weekends and on public holidays, as local tourists from Klang and KL come here to relax and have a seafood meal. There are plenty of eateries, bars and shops, as well as tour operators who can take anglers out on boats for fishing trips or bring tourists to farms where fish, crabs and prawns are reared commercially. End your visit with a meal of fresh seafood, cooked Chinese style, at any of the restaurants on the island. But do bear in mind that clean-liness is also not the island's strongest point. If you are visiting Kuala Selangor *(see p.80)*, note that Pasir Penambang is also a Chinese fishing village, though a more modern one.

PULAU CAREY

In the Mah Meri community on Pulau Carey, the men carve beautiful woodcarvings born of dreams while the womenfolk make traditional woven products. Further on is Jugra, an old capital of Selangor, with a few historical relics that remind us of its royal past.

This is an opportunity to visit what is probably the Klang Valley's last original indigenous woodcarvers' village, located in an oil palm plantation on Pulau Carey (Carey Island).

KAMPUNG SUNGAI BUMBON

About 9km (5½ miles) after turning into Pulau Carey is **Kampung Sungai Bumbon ❶**, home to the Mah Meri (pronounced 'hma meri') Orang Asli people, one of the two indigenous tribes in Peninsular Malaysia who are traditional woodcarvers. Like all traditional Orang Asli, the Mah Meri are animists who worship spirits and conduct ancient ancestral ceremonies. With modern education and influences from the external world, they now speak the Bahasa Malaysia language and many now work in plantations and in the cities. However, the beauty of their heritage lives on in their intricate, unique spirit masks and sculptures.

Dream Designs

According to talented Mah Meri head woodcarver Pion anak Bumbon, the woodcraving designs are said to be revealed to him in his dreams. Aficionados of indigenous art use his

DISTANCE 60km (37 miles) southwest of KL. Pulau Carey to Jugra is about 20km (12½ miles)
TIME Half a day
START Pulau Carey
END Jugra
POINTS TO NOTE
Hire a taxi from KL (RM20–25 per hour). The taxi will take the Lebuhraya Shah Alam (Kesas Highway E5) to Klang; exit at Pandamaran and turn left onto Route 5 towards Banting. To continue with this excursion after tour 16 (Klang), take a taxi from the Klang KTM Komuter station and get onto Route 5 towards Banting; you pass the Kesas Interchange. After about 14km (9 miles), you reach Teluk Panglima Garang and a roundabout. Follow the signs to Pulau Carey. After 1km (½ mile), look out for a sharp right turn: this road takes you across a bridge to Pulau Carey.

works as reference, or consult a tome on Mah Meri culture that was put together by a German researcher years ago, which documents the different types of masks and sculptures with photographs. Interestingly, the book also doubles as a sales catalogue, as the

Ari' Muyang

Held one month after Chinese New Year, Ari' Muyang (Ancestor's Day Celebration) is an excellent time to visit Kampung Sungai Bumbon. Family altars are decorated and offerings are made. The shaman leads a ceremony at an ancestral spirit house and a celebratory dance is performed by masked dancers. A feast ends the celebration. There are usually many tourists during this time; the event is worth watching.

Above from left:
intricate weaving; the
Putra Mosque sits on
the edge of the huge
Putrajaya Lake.

Woven Products
Mah Meri traditional
woven products
include finely woven
bujam pouches to
carry betelnuts, but
these have been
modified for modern
use as purses and
handphone pouches.
Less fine weaving
features in mats
and unique *dudo duri*
baskets with folds that
look like thorns.

Demonstrations
If you want to see
craft demonstrations
and performances,
call Maznah
Unyon (mobile tel:
019-609 6164) a
few days ahead.

carvings are also available for sale.
Preservationists fear that tourism and
commercialism may contaminate the
delicate Mah Meri culture, but some
feel this could be the only way the
woodcarving tradition can live on.

In the woodcarving centre, crafts-
men and their masks and sculptures
in various stages of completion sit
among the woodchips. All the carvers
are men; the women do the finishing.
A trademark Mah Meri sculpture is
the *Muyang Tenong Jerat Harimau*, a
monkey and chain ensemble. 'Muyang'
is the Mah Meri term for 'spirit', of
which there are reputedly over 100.

Buy a copy of the English-language
book, *Chita' Hae*, an excellent docu-
mentation of the Mah Meri's oral
history that was produced by the
Tompoq Topoh Mah Meri Women's
'First Weave' Project. The group has
revived the nearly extinct art of
weaving, and their products are on sale.

For lunch or dinner, return to the
bridge. To the left of the bridge on the
mainland side is a good choice, **Kang
Guan Restaurant**, see ⑪①.

JUGRA

Head back onto Route 5 and turn right
at the sign to Jenjarom for **Jugra ❷**,
an old capital of Selangor. All that is
left from the glorious days are a grave-
yard and two historical buildings from
the early 20th century, a mosque and
palace. The **Sultan Abdul Samad
Royal Mausoleum** (daily 9am–5pm;
free; make sure your arms and legs are
covered) is atop a hill and houses the
graves of the former ruler and his
family. The **Istana Bandar** palace
(closed to the public unless the care-
taker is around), built by Sultan Abdul
Samad's son Sultan Alauddin Sulaiman Shah, shows some European
influences. It is now abandoned but is
still attractive. The minarets and arches
of the **Masjid Sultan Alauddin Shah**
(daily 9am–5pm, except prayer times)
bear Mughal architectural elements.

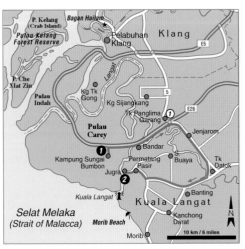

Food and Drink 🍴

① **KANG GUAN
RESTAURANT**
3 Batu 1½, Jalan Bandar Lama,
Telok Panglima Garang; tel: 03-3122
7737; Mon–Fri noon–2.30pm and
6–11pm, Sat–Sun noon–4pm
and 6–11pm; $$
Home-cooked Hokkien food at this
breezy, mangrove-facing eatery.
Recommended are the soft-shelled
crab, fish fillet in mango sauce and
buttered prawns.

PUTRAJAYA

A tribute to Malaysia's period of plenty, the administrative capital of Putrajaya is astounding for the size of its public buildings, monuments and spaces. It looks best when lit up at night and when it hosts colourful events like the National Day Parade.

Conceived in the 1990s by the former Prime Minister Mahathir Mohamad as his mega *pièce de résistance*, **Putrajaya** (www.ppj.gov.my) embodies the huge aspirations – literally – of a nation drunk on a decade of 10 percent GNP growth rates per annum. Named after the country's first prime minister, Tunku Abdul Rahman Putra al-Haj, and covering 4,900ha (12,200 acres), Putrajaya impacts with the sheer scale of its government buildings, public spaces and bridges. Inevitably, it has plenty of detractors, who criticise its lavishness. Others decry its claims to a Muslim heritage, pointing out that the result is more Middle Eastern than local Malay.

PRECINCT 1

On the other hand, however, Putrajaya is a brilliant showcase of postmodern architecture and urban planning. Its centrepiece is **Presint 1** (Precinct 1), from which the rest of the capital radiates. At the heart of Presint 1 is a hill, around which are government offices and the largest artificial wetlands in the tropics. On the hill sits the **Mercu Tanda ❶** (Putrajaya Landmark), a steel sculpture that symbolises the city's beginnings and contains a time

DISTANCE Putrajaya is 25km (15½ miles) south of KL; the tour itself covers 4½km (2¾ miles)
TIME Half a day
START Mercu Tanda
END Taman Botani
POINTS TO NOTE
Start in the late afternoon so you see Putrajaya at night when it looks best. Take the KLIA Transit (20 minutes) from KL Sentral. From the station, hop onto any Nadi Putra bus (50 sen); all buses from the station go to the attractions featured in this tour. The most convenient way around, though, is to hire a taxi.

Drivers Beware
If you are driving, be warned that Putrajaya is not an easy area to navigate as the landscape is pretty uniform, the names of places are very similar and signposting is poor.

Left: futuristic lamp-post design on Putrajaya Boulevard.

Wetland Wonder
You can see a section of Putrajaya's man-made wetland system at the Taman Wetland (Wetland Park; tel: 03-8889 4373; daily 7am–7pm; free). Its Nature Interpretation Centre (daily 9.30am–6pm; free) also has good exhibits on the wetland and its wildlife.

capsule. The sculpture stands among gazebos and fountains in a park, the **Taman Putra Perdana** (Mon–Fri 7am–8pm, Sat, Sun and public holidays 7am–10pm; free).

From this point extends a 4.2-km (2.6-mile) long boulevard, **Persiaran Perdana**, which is the city's spine that links four squares and two bridges. Each National Day (31 August), this boulevard hosts colourful parades.

DATARAN PUTRA

From Taman Putra Perdana, get onto the one-way road that loops around the hill, Persiaran Sultan Salahuddin Abdul Aziz Shah. Head towards **Per-**

dana Putra ❷, the prime minister's office in Kompleks A. You pass an **Information Centre** in Kompleks B (tel: 03-8888 7272; Mon–Sat 8.30am–6.30pm, Sun and public holidays 8.30am–7pm). However, it is poorly staffed, so before you visit Putrajaya, check event listings with Tourism Malaysia (www.tourism.gov.my).

Turn left before Perdana Putra at a sign that points to **Dataran Putra ❸**. This square is actually a circular space with a star-shaped centrepiece representing the country's states; the circle symbolises unity. This is where you get the best view of the green-roofed Perdana Putra. Built in French palatial style, it has an onion-shaped main dome adorned with glazed mosaic, a replica of that of Masjid Zahir, an important mosque in the northern state of Kedah.

PUTRA BRIDGE

Walk down to the **Putra Bridge ❹**. The 435-m (1,430-ft) bridge, with decorative arches and pavilions, was inspired by the well-known 17th-century Khaju Bridge in Isfahan, Iran. It leads to Presint 2 and 3, which hosts other government buildings.

PUTRAJAYA LAKE

Otherwise, turn back to the square, keeping to its left side. Look out for stairs leading down to the **Souq**, a souvenir marketplace, and the **Selera Putra**, see ⑪① and ⑪②, where you can have a drink and a snack. This is

[Map]

- Kuala Lumpur
- Seri Perdana Complex ★
- Tasik Taman Botani (Botanic Gardens)
- Putrajaya ③
- Istana Melawati ★
- TAMAN PUTRA PERDANA
- Government Complex Parcel E ★
- Seri Perdana Bridge
- Mercu Tandu (Putrajaya Landmark) ❶
- PRECINCT 1
- Alamanda ★
- Perdana Putra (Prime Minister's Office) ❷
- ℹ
- ★ Government Complex Parcel D
- Masjid Putra (Putra Mosque) ❻
- Kompleks Jab. Perdana Menteri ★
- ★ Government Complex Parcel C
- ❶❷❸
- Dataran Putra ❹
- Seri Bakti Bridge
- Cruise Tasik Putrajaya ❺
- Putra Bridge
- (Putrajaya Lake)
- ★ Taman Wawasan
- ★ Jab. Akauntan Negara
- ★ Jab. Kastam Diraja Malaysia
- Seri Wawasan Bridge
- ★ Perbendaharaan Malaysia
- ★ Kementerian Kewangan Malaysia
- Kementerian Pembangunan Usahawan
- PRECINCT 2
- Jab. P. ★ Negara
- ★ KPDN & HEP   PRECINCT 18
- ★ Kementerian Perusahaan Periadangan
- ★ Kompleks Perbadanan Putrajaya
- ★ Palace of Justice
- PRECINCT 3
- N
- 1000 m / 1100 yds

also where you find the jetty for **Cruise Tasik Putrajaya** ❺ (tel: 03-8888 5539; daily 9am–7pm; charge; www.cruisetasikputrajaya.com), which offers 25-minute gondola rides (daily 10am–6.30pm) or 45-minute cruise boat rides (hourly departures Mon–Fri 1–6pm, Sat, Sun and public holidays 11am–7pm) on **Tasik Putrajaya** (Putrajaya Lake). The sunset cruise is worth taking (7pm on weekends only).

PUTRA MOSQUE

Go back up to the square to visit its star attraction, the **Masjid Putra** ❻ (Putra Mosque; tel: 03-8888 5678; daily 9am–12.30pm, 3–4pm and 5.30–6pm; free). The mosque features 16th to 18th-century Persian Islamic architecture, with rose-tinted granite mosaic as tile decorations. Its main entrance is fashioned after public gates in Muslim Persia. Three-quarters of the mosque extends out onto the lake, so it looks like it is 'floating' on water.

BOTANICAL GARDENS

Leave the square and get back onto Persiaran Sultan Salahudin Abdul Aziz Shah. About 3km (1¼ miles) on is the turn-off to **Taman Botani** ❼ (Botanical Gardens; tel: 03-8888 9090; daily 7am–7pm; charge for some attractions). Stroll, cycle or take a tram ride (charge) through its diverse botanical collections, which includes a Sun Garden with a sundial. The elaborate Moroccan Pavilion (charge) features replicas of architecture found in four historical Moroccan cities. End the day with dinner at the lakeside **Putrajaya Seafood Restaurant**, see ③.

Above from far left: Perdana Putra, the prime minister's office; sunset cruise.

Brilliant Architecture In Presint 3 are two magnificent buildings. The Kompleks Perbadanan Putrajaya (Putrajaya Corporation Complex) has an awe-inspiring contemporary Islamic gateway *(below left)*, while the Istana Kehakiman (Palace of Justice) has Mughal-influenced features. You need a car to get there.

Food and Drink

① **LA CUCUR**
S03 Selera Putra, Presint 1; tel: 03-2694 6920; daily 8am–8pm; $
This chain serves a nice variety of Malay and Nonya *kuih* (cakes); try the banana-based *kuih bengkang* and *kuih talam* steamed pudding.

② **KELLY'S CAFÉ**
S05 Selera Putra, Presint 1; mobile tel: 012-506 0878; daily 9am–9pm; $
Cool down with ice-blended fruit juices or the huge rainbow-coloured and ice-cream-topped *ice kacang*, a local desert of shaved ice with red beans and corn.

③ **PUTRAJAYA SEAFOOD RESTAURANT**
Taman Botani Putrajaya, Presint 1; tel: 03-8889 1188; daily noon–2.30pm and 6–10.30pm; $$
In this delightful lakeside setting, enjoy signature dishes such as Thai seafood claypot and deep-fried abalone mushroom.

DIRECTORY

A user-friendly alphabetical listing of practical information,
plus hand-picked hotels and restaurants, clearly organised
by area, to suit all budgets and tastes.

A

ADDRESSES

All road signs and place names are in Bahasa Malaysia (Malay) but many also appear in English. In this guidebook we have chosen to use the names that are most commonly used by the locals – sometimes it is English and sometimes Malay. Note that the lowest two floors of multistorey buildings are usually referred to as the ground floor (G/F) and the first floor (1/F). As Chinese associate the number '4' with death, in some lifts, the fourth floor button is marked as '3A' instead.

B

BUDGETING

KL is a bargain, particularly in off-peak seasons. If you are frugal, you can get by on RM120 a day; RM200 per day is a fair budget.

Decent budget accommodation starts at RM60; on average, RM250–300 gets you a room in a good 4-star hotel. Many hotels include breakfast with the room rate.

Street food is very cheap; a meal with a soft drink can be as low as RM7. Generally, budget RM30 for a main meal. Alcohol is very expensive, with beers going for RM10–14 a pop, so do take advantage of Happy Hours. Admission fees for attractions and theatre tickets are generally reasonable, and matinee theatre shows are discounted. Public transport is cheap, but taxis may charge double by insisting on a flat rate during peak hours and levy a 50 percent surcharge between midnight and 6am. Car hire is reasonably priced, but parking in the city centre and in 5-star hotels is very expensive.

BUSINESS HOURS

Government offices and some private businesses operate Monday–Friday 8.30am–5.30pm, with a one-hour lunch break from 12.30pm. There is a longer lunch break from 12.45–2.45pm for Muslim prayers on Friday. Some companies operate on Saturday 9am–1pm.

During the Muslim fasting month of Ramadan, government office hours are Monday–Thursday 8am–4.30pm and Friday 8am–4pm. Hours for private businesses vary, though most retain the same hours.

Banking hours are Monday–Friday 9.30am–4pm, although banks in shopping malls and areas like Masjid India, the Golden Triangle, Jalan Ampang and Bangsar open 10am–7pm on weekdays and 10am–1pm on Saturday. Money-changing kiosks in the city are open till 7pm daily. Shops and department stores open Monday–Saturday 9–11am and close 9–10pm, and Sunday 10am–8pm.

Restaurants usually open from 11am–2.30pm and 5–11pm while café hours are 7am–10pm. They close later on weekends. *Mamak* outlets that serve Indian and Malay food are open 24 hours a day; some hawker places only open for dinner and close at 4am.

C

CHILDREN

The city is not baby-friendly – facilities for breast-feeding, nappy-changing and pushchairs are inadequate. Some hotels with 4 stars and above have kids' clubs, with activities and minders for children. Malls and fast-food outlets have play areas.

Children may be more susceptible to heat and food- and water-related ailments. Always use sunblock, hats, insect repellent and drink lots of water. While pharmacies, such as Watsons and Guardian, are well stocked with children's medication, do bring along any special medication.

CLIMATE

Malaysia's weather is generally hot and humid all year round, with temperatures ranging from 32°C (89.6°F) during the day to 22°C (71.6°F) at night. It is slightly colder in the highlands like Fraser's Hill and Genting Highlands. Humidity is at 80 percent; quick showers and thunderstorms occasionally occur. The heaviest rainfall is during the inter-monsoon periods of April to May and October to November. The months of January to March are hot and dry.

Thick haze has been recurrent in recent years, from July to October, with most of the smoke blown in from parts of Indonesia hit by forest fires.

Weather patterns have become unpredictable. Check for more details with the Malaysian Meteorological Service (www.kjc.gov.my).

CLOTHING

Pack cottons and natural fibres, sunglasses, sunblock and umbrellas. Shoes are removed before one enters temples and homes, so slip-ons are handy.

CRIME AND SECURITY

Snatch and petty thefts are common. Snatch thieves tend to consist of two men on a motorcycle or men leaning out of moving cars. If your bag is snatched, give in, as many thieves carry knives, which they will not hesitate to use. Always walk in the direction of oncoming traffic and make sure your bag is on the side away from traffic. If you do not want to leave your valuables and passport in the hotel room safe, leave them with the reception. At night, keep to well-lit areas.

The Tourist Police (tel: 03-2149 6590), who patrol tourist spots, can help with lost passports and give general advice. You can also get help at any police station or booth (tel: 999).

CUSTOMS

You must declare all prohibited and dutiable goods. The former includes drugs, dangerous chemicals, pornography, firearms and ammunition. Note that possession of drugs carries a death sentence. Items such as cameras, watches, pens, perfumes, cosmetics and lighters are duty free. You may have to

Women Travellers

It is generally safe for women to travel alone in KL. Wearing a wedding band, or just saying, 'Yes, I'm married,' in reply to queries on marriage status, are two ways of preventing further interest. For unsolicited attention, be polite but firm and walk away if you are uncomfortable. Clothes that are too revealing will draw stares. You should dress more conservatively in places of worship and outside the city. Topless bathing at swimming pools is prohibited.

pay a deposit for temporary importation of dutiable goods – usually 30 percent of the value. This is refundable on departure (keep your receipt of purchase and get an official receipt for any tax or deposit paid). For details, call the **Customs Department** at tel: 03-8882 2000; www.customs.gov.my.

D

DISABLED TRAVELLERS

Basic disabled-friendly facilities, like extra-wide parking bays and toilets, and wheelchair ramps, are found in major hotels, malls, theatres, fast-food restaurants and some government buildings. KLIA and the Light Rail Transit (LRT) system are also disabled-friendly. But in general, KL falls short with uneven pavements, potholes and unsympathetic drivers. Taxis will usually not transport people in wheelchairs.

E

EMBASSIES

Australia: 6 Jalan Yap Kwan Seng; tel: 03-2146 5555; www.australia.org.my
Canada: 17/F, Menara Tan & Tan, 207 Jalan Tun Razak; tel: 03-2718 3333; www.dfaitmaeci.gc.ca/kualalumpur
Ireland: The Amp Walk, 218 Jalan Ampang; tel: 03-2161 2963; www.ireland-embassy.com.my
New Zealand: 21/F, Menara IMC, 8 Jalan Sultan Ismail; tel: 03-2078 2533; www.nzembassy.com
UK: 185 Jalan Ampang; tel: 03-2170 2200; www.britain.org.my
US: 376 Jalan Tun Razak; tel: 03-2168 5000; malaysia.usembassy.gov

EMERGENCIES

Police/Fire Brigade/Civil Defence: 999 (112 from mobile phone)

ETIQUETTE

Greetings: It is considered rude to address older people by their names. Unless you know your business associates well or you know otherwise, always use titles such as Mr (Encik), Madam (Mrs) or Ms (Cik).

Men must never offer to shake a Muslim lady's hand unless she offers it first. A simple nod or smile will suffice. Similar rules apply to women wanting to shake a Muslim man's hand. A limp handshake is actually a Malay greeting *(salam)*, which involves brushing the palm of the other person and placing the hand on one's heart. This signifies 'I am pleased to meet you from the bottom of my heart'.

Head & Feet: The Hindu religion regards the head as the wellspring of wisdom and the feet as unclean, so it is insulting to touch another adult's head, point one's feet at anything, or step over another person. Malays consider it rude to point the index finger at something; make a fist with the right hand and the thumb folded on top, and then aim at the subject. If entering a home, remove your shoes. It is courteous to bring a gift, no matter how

Electricity
Electrical outlets are rated at 220 volts, 50 cycles, and serve three-pin, flat-pronged plugs. American products do not work here, but most supermarkets stock adapters. Major hotels can supply an adapter for 110–120 volt, 60 Hz appliances.

small. Never refuse drinks or snacks served to you, even if it is to take just a sip or bite. In a Malay home, when passing in front of someone, bow slightly while walking and point an arm down to indicate the path to be taken.

Places of Worship: Remove your shoes before entering. At the mosque, non-Muslims are prohibited from entering certain areas; signs are clearly displayed. Conservative clothing covering arms and legs is advisable.

Certain Hindu temples are not open to non-Hindus to keep the place 'untainted' from people who consume beef. If you enter a Sikh temple, be sure to cover your hair. Be sensitive about photographing worshippers in prayer.

Public Behaviour: Public displays of affection other than hand-holding is considered bad form, especially if you are with a local or look like one. Shouting and talking loudly, even outside a nightspot, is considered rude.

G

GAY AND LESBIAN

KL has a sizeable gay community, unofficially estimated at 60,000. Malaysian society is generally tolerant of alternative lifestyles – though not of public displays of affection – and appreciative of the pink dollar. Gay visitors can travel safely and without fear of persecution in KL, usually facing only minor harassment from police, if it even happens at all. However, note

that there are provisions in the Penal Code, and for Muslims, Islamic Shar'iah laws, that penalise same-sex sexual acts and cross-dressing.

Comprehensive information is available on the gay portal Utopia at www.utopia-asia.com/tipsmala.htm.

GOVERNMENT

Malaysia is a constitutional monarchy with executive power vested in the prime minister and legislative power in an elected parliament. The government comprises a coalition of political parties (Barisan Nasional) that has ruled the country since independence. KL is a Federal Territory and the legislative capital; it is administered locally by a City Hall, led by a mayor.

H

HEALTH

Visitors entering Malaysia are not required to show evidence of vaccination for smallpox or cholera, but it is a good idea to immunise yourself against cholera, hepatitis A and B and tetanus. There are periodic outbreaks of dengue fever for which there is no immunisation, so take preventive measures like using insect repellent, especially outside of the city areas. If you suffer from a very high fever while (or shortly after) visiting Malaysia, consult a doctor immediately.

Note that the haze *(see p.99)* affects those with respiratory illnesses, especially asthmatics. Stay indoors or wear

Above from far left: the massive Putra Bridge; National Monument at Lake Gardens; Putra Mosque in Putrajaya; Barisan Nasional flags.

a mask when outdoors. The risk of bird flu in Malaysia is believed to be very low, but as a precaution, avoid visiting live animal markets and poultry farms, and ensure poultry and egg dishes are thoroughly cooked.

Make sure you drink at least 2 litres (8–10 glasses) of water to keep hydrated. Avoid the sun during the hottest part of the day (11am–1pm). Drink only boiled or bottled water. Avoid ice cubes at streetside stalls and small coffee shops, as they are usually made with unboiled water. Refrain from eating peeled fruit from street stalls. Otherwise, food served in restaurants and at hawker centres is clean.

Hospitals: All major hotels have an on-premise clinic or a doctor-on-call. KL offers advanced medical care in both government and private hospitals. Government hospitals charge a fraction of what private ones demand, but there is usually a longer waiting time.
Hospital KL: Jalan Pahang; tel: 03-2615 5555; www.hkl.gov.my
Tung Shin Hospital: Jalan Pudu (near Puduraya); tel: 03-2072 1655; www.tungshinhospital.com.my
Gleneagles Intan Medical Centre: Jalan Ampang; tel: 03-4257 1300; www.gimc.com.my

Medical Clinics: For minor problems, there are many private clinics around the city, some open 24 hours.

Pharmacies: Pharmacies are found everywhere, especially in malls, usually operated by chains like Watsons and Guardian. A licensed pharmacist is on duty on weekdays 10am–5pm. A prescription is required for controlled drugs. Check the expiry dates.
Dental Clinics: Dental clinics are found in hospitals, major shopping malls and shopping areas like Bukit Bintang and KLCC. Consultancy rates start at RM30.
Dentalpro Dental Specialist Centre: 8 Lengkok Abdullah, Bangsar Utama; tel: 03-2287 3333
Pristine Dental Clinic: F-074, 2/F, Mid Valley Megamall; tel: 03-2287 3782
Twin Towers Medical Centre KLCC: 401 F&G, 4/F, Suria KLCC; tel: 03-2382 3500

I

INTERNET

Broadband internet access is available in the city, the airport and hotels of all categories. Wireless broadband (Wi-fi) is becoming widespread. In cafés, Wi-fi is usually free with the purchase of food or drinks; the cashier will give you a log-in name and password. Internet cafés are found in shopping areas like Petaling Street and KLCC; rates start from RM2 per hour.

L

LEFT LUGGAGE

Hotels usually provide free left luggage services for their guests. **KLIA** (tel: 03-8776 6035) has locker rental services in

---

Lost Property
If you have lost your property or passport, call the Tourist Police at 03-2149 6590 or lodge a report at the nearest police station. For lost property at KLIA, call the KLIA police booth, Level 5, Main Building (tel:03-8776 3450); for left luggage on the aircraft or missing check-in baggage, call KLIA Information (tel: 03-8776 4386/89). For lost property at KL Sentral, call Information (tel: 03-2730 2000).

the Satellite Building, and arrival and departure halls of the main building. **KL Sentral** (tel: 03-2730 2000) has lockers on Levels 1 and 2. There are also left luggage services at **Puduraya** bus station (tel: 03-2070 0145).

M

MEDIA

Newspapers/Magazines: Malaysia's English-language dailies include *The Star*, *The New Straits Times*, *The Sun*, *The Edge* and *Malay Mail*. Major hotels provide free local English-language dailies every morning, or you can purchase them at any bookshop, news-stand or convenience store. You can also buy *The Wall Street Journal*, *The International Herald Tribune*, *USA Today*, as well as international periodicals and magazines at bookshops and hotel news-stands. *Juice*, *KLue* and *Faces* magazines are good for entertainment listings.

Radio: English-language news is broadcast hourly on stations such as Hitz 92.9, which plays mainly American hits; Mix 94.5, which plays a mixture of new and old hits; and Light 105.7, which plays retro and classics. The government-run Traxx 90.3 airs a mix of music and talk shows.

Television: Cable TV, with channels such as CNN, BBC and HBO, is available in most hotels. Free-to-air local TV stations are run by RTM (TV1 and TV2) and by private stations TV3, NTV7, 8TV and 9TV. All except for TV1 have news reports in English and American programmes. The paid satellite TV operator Astro has as many as 100 channels.

MONEY

Currency: The Malaysian ringgit (RM) is divided into 100 sen. Bank notes are in units of 1, 2, 5, 10, 50 and 100, and coins are in 1-, 5-, 10-, 20- and 50-sen denominations.

ATMs: Local ATMs, found in shopping areas and centres, operate 6am–midnight but some international banks operate 24-hour machines. You can use your credit card to withdraw money from these machines; check with your credit card companies for location details of these ATMs.

Currency Exchange: Money-changers are located everywhere, including the main bus and train terminals. Banks and Bureau de Change at KLIA charge a commission but money-changers do not. Try bargaining; larger amounts get you better rates.

Credit Cards: These are widely accepted in major shopping malls, hotels and petrol stations. Note that some retailers add an extra 2–3 percent surcharge – so ask first before paying. Be aware of credit card fraud.
American Express: 03-2050 0000
Diners: 03-2161 1055 (office hours), 03-2161 2862 (after office hours)
MasterCard: 1800-804 594

Above from far left: food is readily available all hours of the day; wireless broadband access at an internet café.

Maps
Basic maps are available free at most hotels. You can also purchase decent maps from any good bookshop or convenience store. The *Insight Fleximap KL* is a good one to get.

Visa: 1800-802 997

Traveller's Cheques: Traveller's cheques are accepted but are not commonly used; the best rates are offered by banks.

Taxes and Tipping: Most services are subject to a 10 percent service charge and a 5 percent government tax. These are listed on your bills; if not, you are welcome to tip.

Porters are tipped RM2–5, restaurant and bar staff are usually left loose change or change from bills rounded off to the nearest 10. Feel free to tip more for good service. Taxi drivers are usually not tipped.

P

PHOTOGRAPHY

Camera shops are widely found in malls and tourist areas. Cameras and accessories are good bargains, as they are duty free here. Most photo-processing shops offer digital photo transfers into CD and print services. For camera repairs and second-hand equipment, head to the Pudu area. Likewise, video equipment and digital tapes are affordable.

Be prepared for rain and always have a plastic bag handy for your equipment. Note that the humidity in rainforested areas can damage cameras. Pack a dry non-lint cloth for wiping your camera. Although there are no restrictions on what you can photograph or video, use your discretion in religious places. When in doubt, ask for permission. Some attractions charge a fee for cameras.

POSTAL SERVICES

Pos Malaysia (tel: 1300-300 300; www.pos.com.my) offers a gamut of services, including registered mail, parcels and courier services (Poslaju), as well as the cashing of postal and money orders. Most post offices are open Monday–Friday 8am–5.30pm. The **General Post Office** (Monday–Saturday 8.30am–4.30pm) is at Kompleks Dayabumi. Post offices with extended hours from Monday to Saturday are in Bangsar (until 10pm), Mid Valley Megamall (until 6pm), Suria KLCC (until 6pm) and Sungei Wang Plaza (until 6pm). There is also a post office in the Main Building in KLIA (Monday–Saturday 8.30am–5.30pm).

International courier services include: **Federal Express (FedEx):** The Weld Shopping Centre, Jalan Raja Chulan; tel: 1800-886 363; Monday–Friday 10am–7pm and Saturday 10am–2pm. **United Parcel Services (UPS and DHL):** Mail Boxes Etc., A-G-3A Ground Floor, Mid Valley (near Boulevard Hotel); tel: 03-2282 7622; Monday–Friday 9am–7pm, Saturday 10am–2pm.

PUBLIC HOLIDAYS

Some holidays are fixed while others have variable dates as they are governed by the lunar calendar. Check specific dates with **Tourism Malaysia** (tel: 1300-885 050; www.tourism.gov.my).
New Year's Day: 1 January
Thaipusam: end January
Federal Territory Day: 1 February

Chinese New Year: January/February
Labour Day: 1 May
Wesak Day: May
Agong's (King's) Birthday: first Saturday in June
National Day: 31 August
Deepavali: October/November
Christmas: 25 December
Prophet Muhammad's Birthday: date varies
Hari Raya Puasa: date varies
Hari Raya Haji: date varies

R

RELIGION

As the majority of the population are Muslim, mosques are very common and all public buildings have at least a *surau* (prayer room). There are also ample places of worship for Buddhists, Taoists, Hindus, Sikhs and followers of other faiths. Of the various Christian denominations, here is a list of churches that offer English-language services.
Anglican: St Mary's Cathedral: Jalan Raja; tel: 03-2692 8672
Catholic: Cathedral of St John: 5 Jalan Bukit Nanas; tel: 03-2078 1876
Methodist: Wesley Methodist Church; 2 Jalan Wesley (near Puduraya); tel: 03-2072 0338

T

TELEPHONES

Phone Numbers: IDD (International Direct Dial) phones are available in guest rooms. To call abroad directly, first dial the international access code 00, followed by the country code.

Dial 103 (30 sen per call) for local and international telephone directory assistance, and for operator-assisted calls, dial 101 (70 sen per local call, RM2 per international call). To call KL from overseas, dial the international country code 60 for Malaysia, followed by 3, the area code for KL and Selangor; 9 for Pahang.

Public Phones: The cost of a local call on a public payphone is 10 sen per 3 minutes. Payphones maintained in shops and restaurants charge twice or three times that amount.

Mobile Phones: Malaysia mobile phones use the GSM network. If your phone has a roaming facility, it will automatically hook up to a local network. Otherwise, prepaid SIM cards are very affordable, starting at RM20 for registration and airtime.

Prepaid Phone Cards: Calls may also be made using prepaid phone cards, which come in denominations of RM5–100. They can be purchased from phone shops, convenience stores and news-stands.

TOURIST INFORMATION

For detailed and comprehensive information and updates, visit the **Tourism Malaysia** website at www.tourism.gov.my, or call the infoline, tel: 1300-885 050. Tourist offices have helpful staff and ample brochures and maps.

Time Zone
Malaysian time is 8 hours ahead of GMT and 16 hours ahead of US Pacific Standard Time.

Toilets
Public restrooms can be dirty and wet, and many still have squat toilets. Toilet paper is not always available, although you can sometimes buy small tissue packs at the entrance. Most malls charge an entrance fee of 20–50 sen. If you are concerned, stick to using hotel toilets.

Visitor Service Centre, KLIA: Arrival Hall, Level 3, Main Building; daily 24 hours; tel: 03-8776 5647

Malaysia Tourism Centre: 109 Jalan Ampang; daily 8am–10pm, tel: 03-9235 4848; www.mtc.gov.my

Tourism Malaysia Headquarters: 17/F, Menara Dato' Onn, Putra World Trade Centre, Jalan Tun Ismail; Monday–Friday 8.30am–5pm; tel: 03-2615 8188

KL Sentral: 2/F, Arrival Halls, Kuala Lumpur City Air Terminal; daily 9am–6pm; tel: 03-2272 5823

Overseas Offices

Australia: Level 2, 171 Clarence Street, Sydney; tel: 61-2-9299 4441

Canada: 1590–1111, West Georgia Street, Vancouver; tel: 60-4-689 8899; www.tourismmalaysia.ca

UK: 57 Trafalgar Square, London; tel: 44-20-7930 7932

US: 120 East 56th Street, Suite 810, New York; tel: 1-212-754 1113

For a full list of offices, visit www.tourism.gov.my.

TOURS

Most hotels offer their own shuttle bus or van tours around the city. Some might not be licensed, so ask your hotel concierge or the reception desk to recommend a reliable tour company. Half-day 3-hour city tours are priced at RM44–65 per person. Full-day tours of 8 hours cost RM200–220 per person.

Individual tour guides charge a per-hour fee. Be sure to use the services of a licensed guide. Call the **KL Tour** Guide Association (tel: 03-9221 0688).

The following tour agencies offer tours of KL and its environs as well as longer and more comprehensive tours of various destinations in Malaysia.

Asian Overland Services: tel: 03-4252 9100; www.asianoverland.com.my

Holiday Tours & Travel: tel: 03-2719 1800; www.holidaytours.com.my

Mayflower Acme Tours: tel: 03-6252 1888; www.mayflower.com.my

Diethelm Travel: tel: 03-2715 7878; www.diethelmtravel.com

Sri America Travel Corporation: tel: 03-2142 9155

TRANSPORT

Arrival

By Air: Kuala Lumpur International Airport, or KLIA (tel: 03-8776 4386/89; www.klia.com.my), is located 70km (43 miles) south of the city in Sepang. Planes arrive at and depart from four satellite arms, which are linked to the main terminal building via a convenient aerotrain with departures at 3–5-minute intervals.

The national carrier is **Malaysia Airlines** (MAS) (24-hour call centre tel: 03-7843 3000 or 1300-883 000 toll-free within Malaysia; www.malaysia airlines.com), which flies to over 100 international and domestic destinations. Its subsidiary, **Firefly**, operates small Fokker 50 planes to selected local destinations (tel: 03-7845 4543; daily 8am–9pm; www.fireflyz.com.my). Local budget airline **AirAsia** (tel: 03-8775 4000 8am–9pm, toll-free within Malaysia; www.airasia.com) offers

KL Hop-On Hop-Off

Plying 22 stops around the city, this double-decker bus service runs every 30–45 min from 8.30am–8.30pm daily. You can get on and off the bus at any of the designated stops along the way. Pre-recorded commentary is available on the bus. One-day tickets at RM38 for adults and RM17 for children and senior citizens can be purchased on the bus itself, at selected hotels and travel agents or online at www.myhoponhopoff.com. For inquiries call Elang Wah Sdn Bhd at tel: 03-2691 1382.

cheap fares to both domestic and regional destinations. Check online for discounted fares.

MAS flights depart from KLIA while AirAsia flights depart from the **Low Cost Carrier Terminal** (LCC-T) (tel: 03-8777 8888; www.klia.com.my/ LCCTerminal), located some 20km (12 miles) from KLIA. Feeder buses running at 20-minute intervals link the two terminals. Firefly flies from the **Sultan Abdul Aziz Shah Airport** or **Subang**, 20km (12½ miles) from KL (tel: 03-7836 1833).

Airport Transfers: The fastest way from KLIA to the city centre is by the **KLIA Express** train (daily 5am–midnight; tel: 03-2267 8000; www.klia ekspres.com), which takes 28 minutes to get to KL Sentral station (RM35). If you are flying with MAS, Cathay Pacific or Royal Brunei for the return trip, you can do a flight check-in, including luggage, at the **Central Air Terminal** (CAT) at KL Sentral 2–12 hours before departure. Alternative transport modes are **Airport Limo** taxis (tel: 03-8787 3030; 24 hours; buy a coupon before leaving the airport) and **Airport Coach** (tel: 03-6203 3067; daily 6.15am–12.30am).

From LCC-T, the very affordable **Skybus** (www.skybus.com.my; daily 7am–2.30am) goes to KL Sentral, while the **Airport Coach** (tel: 03-6203 3067; daily 5am–12.30am) ferries passengers to Hentian Duta or the Jalan Chan Sow Lin LRT Station. Skyvans take passengers to hotels, and airport taxis go anywhere (tel: 03-8787 4113;

daily 24 hours). City taxis cannot legally pick up passengers at the airport, but you can catch any taxi from the city to the airport – the fare is based on mileage plus a surcharge.

By Rail: The main train line from Singapore to Bangkok and beyond stops at the KL Sentral station. The KTMB (National Railways; tel: 03-2267 1200; www.ktmb.com.my) trains are modern and the service is efficient. Travellers generally take the express services, which make a minimal number of stops. There are three classes of service. Most trains are air-conditioned and have buffet cars serving simple meals. Comfortable sleeping berths are available on long-distance night trains.

There are day and night trains to both Singapore and Butterworth in Penang. From Butterworth, there are train connections to Thailand. Ask about the **Visit Malaysia Rail Pass** (5, 10 or 15 days), which can be used on all Peninsular Malaysia services.

By Road: The North-South Expressway, which stretches from southern Peninsular Malaysia to the Thai border, provides a convenient means of travel through the peninsula, the entire trip taking about 12 hours by car one way. There are two links from Singapore: across the Causeway from Woodlands to Johor Bahru, and Linke Dua (Second Link) from Tuas to Tanjung Kupang. Try to avoid crossing the border on Friday afternoons and during public holidays because the traffic can be heavy at the checkpoints.

Above from far left: Jalan Alor street sign; peak hour passengers.

E&O
The luxurious Eastern and Oriental Express (Singapore tel: 65-6392 3500; www.orient-express.com) travels several times a month between Singapore and Bangkok, making a stop at the Old KL Railway Station on certain days.

Long-distance buses also travel to and from KL to most destinations on the peninsula as well as to Singapore and Thailand. The main inter-state bus stations are at **Puduraya** (tel: 03-2070 0145) near Petaling Street, and **Hentian Putra** in northern KL (tel: 03-4041 4642). The air-conditioned express buses are comfortable, with video entertainment on board. The buses make occasional stops along the expressway for meals and toilet breaks.

Plusliner (tel: 03-2272 1586; www.plusliner.com) picks and drops passengers at the Old KL Railway Station and operates daily coach services to various cities in the peninsula as well as a direct service (4 hours) to Singapore on its executive service with only 24 seats. Another coach service is **Transnasional** (tel: 03-2161 1864; www.nadi.com.my/transportation_home.asp), which stops at all bus terminals.

Long-distance air-conditioned taxis also leave for selected destinations from Puduraya. Share the cost with other passengers to spread out the cost.

By Sea: KL's closest seaport is **Port Klang** (Pelabuhan Klang), about 40km (25 miles) away, and is linked by highways, buses and the KTM Komuter train service. Ferries from Tanjung Balai, Sumatra (in Indonesia) dock here (tel: 03-3167 1058). Port Klang is the main port of call for regional cruise ships and international liners.

Within KL

Taxis: Taxis have a 'Teksi' sign on their roofs, which, when lit, signals avail-ability. They offer a convenient and economical means of moving around the city, and drivers usually speak at least a smattering of English.

Air-conditioning and fare meters are compulsory in all taxis. Make sure the meter is switched on after you get in. Rates are RM2 for the first 2km (1.24 miles) and 10 sen for each additional 160m/yd. There is a surcharge of RM1 for booking a taxi by phone, and a 50 percent surcharge on the meter fare between midnight and 6am. If there are more than two passengers per taxi, 20 sen per additional passenger is levied. There are also premium taxis that have a RM4 flagfall and charge more per kilometre.

You can get a taxi by queueing at taxi stands, flagging one down by the street, or booking one by telephone. During peak hours, some taxis will not go to places where traffic is bad and where passengers are hard to come by on the return leg. In such cases, drivers either decline passengers or will charge a flat rate. If you have to bargain, note that fares around town start at RM5 and it should cost you no more than RM10 to go across the central city area.

Half- and full-day taxi charters to Klang Valley cost RM20–25 per hour, excluding toll charges. You can also book with reliable taxi companies such as **Comfort** (tel: 03-8024 0507) and **Public Cab** (tel: 03-6259 2020); call at least four hours beforehand.

Buses: Several companies provide bus services in KL. Rapid KL's **City Shuttle** buses (tel: 03-7625 6999; www.rapid

Above from far left: scooters at Central Market; the Monorail is an efficient means of public transport.

kl.com.my) cover most major areas in the city and provide feeder services to train (mainly LRT) stations.

The main inner-city bus stops are Puduraya, the Klang Bus Station and Bangkok Bank near Central Market, Lebuh Ampang, and the Jalan Tuanku Abdul Rahman/Jalan Ipoh intersection in Chow Kit. Buses are packed during peak periods; watch your wallets.

Rental Cars: Chauffered limousines are offered by **Avis** (tel: 03-7628 2300), **Kasina Rent-A-Car** (tel: 03-8787 1739) and **Hertz** (tel: 03-2715 8383). Many hotels also provide chauffeured services; do check that they are licensed. For self-drive cars, rental rates vary according to insurance options and vehicle type, but rates generally start at RM150 per day.

Train and Light Rail: KTMB also operates the KTM Komuter (tel: 03-2267 1200; www.ktmb.com.my) electric commuter rail service, which transports commuters and travellers on two lines within greater KL and Klang Valley.

Within the city, the Light Rail Transport (LRT) (tel: 03-7625 6999; www.rapidkl.com.my) has two lines that intersect at Masjid Jamek and services areas such as the Golden Triangle, the old city centre, Chow Kit, Petaling Jaya and Bangsar. The **Monorail** (tel: 03-2267 9888; www.monorail.com.my) covers the Bukit Bintang, Brickfields and Titiwangsa areas. The central hub for all these services is **KL Sentral** (tel: 03-2279 8888; www.stesensentral.com).

V

VISAS AND PASSPORTS

Passports must be valid for at least six months at the time of entry. Visa requirements change from time to time, so check with a Malaysian embassy or consulate or the **Immigration Department** website (www.imi.gov.my) before travelling. Generally, no visa is needed for citizens of Commonwealth countries (with exceptions) and the US (unlimited period); most EU countries (up to three months); and all ASEAN countries except Myanmar and some EU countries (up to one month). Most tourists can get a visa on arrival at the KLIA for a 30-day social visit pass (RM100).

WEBSITES

All Malaysia: www.allmalaysia.info. General site with contents from leading English newspaper, *The Star*.
Fried Chillies: www.friedchillies.com. Reviews of and guide to food in KL.
Journeymalaysia: www.journeymalaysia.com. Comprehensive information related to travel.
Kakiseni: www.kakiseni.com. Listings of contemporary-arts events.
KLue: www.klue.com.my. Listings of entertainment events.
The Other Malaysia: www.othermalaysia.org. Insightful essays on history, politics and culture written by influential intellectual, Farish Noor.

Weights and Measurements
Malaysia uses the metric system, although traditional measurements, such as *kati* (60g) and miles (for distance), are also used.

Historic Heart

Heritage Station Hotel

Bangunan Stesen Keretapi, Jalan Sultan Hishamuddin; tel: 03-2273 5588; www.heritagehotel malaysia.com; $$

Located in the Old KL Railway Station, this hotel was once the place to stay in colonial times. Some fixtures have been retained, including the clanking old lift, historical wall hangings and lovely arched Mughal windows. Rooms and dorms have been modernised, though slightly worn.

Westover Lodge

2/F, 4 Medan Pasar; tel: 03-2070 1286; www.westoverlodge.com; $

This well-run new budget outfit only has 10 rooms, some of which are small and have no windows. That said, the place is spotless, very friendly and has comfortable common areas; strictly no smoking in rooms.

Petaling Street and Surroundings

Ancasa Hotel

Jalan Tun Tan Cheng Lock; tel: 03-2026 6060; www.ancasa-hotel.com; $$

Conveniently located between Petaling Street and the Puduraya bus station, with markets and historical areas close by. Don't expect too much of the service, but the rooms are good value for money.

Hotel Malaya

Jalan Hang Lekir; tel: 03-2072 7722; www.hotelmalaya.com.my; $$

A great location to experience the rhythms of Petaling Street. This 3-star has comfortable rooms. Its restaurant serves delicious Nonya fare.

Le Village

99A Jalan Tun H.S. Lee; mobile tel: 013-355 0235; $

Housed in a century-old shophouse, this simple outfit with a rooftop garden and basic fan-cooled rooms is a stone's throw from the Central Market and public transport. Guests have complimentary use of the kitchen and enjoy free tea and coffee.

Swiss-Inn Kuala Lumpur

62 Jalan Sultan; tel: 03-2072 3333; www.swissgarden.com; $$

Set in an early 20th-century Chinese shophouse, this hotel fronts a street with Chinese eateries and tea shops, while its back opens directly to the Petaling Street bazaar. Rooms, though basic, are clean and value for money.

Kuala Lumpur City Centre

The Ascott

9 Jalan Pinang; tel: 03-2142 6868; www.the-ascott.com; $$$$

This serviced apartment across the KLCC has splendid views of the city from its rooftop pool. Options range from studio to three-bedroom apart-

Price for a double room with breakfast and taxes:	
$$$$	over RM400
$$$	RM300–399
$$	RM100–299
$	below RM100

ments, all with fully equipped kitchens and facilities that cater to families and business folk.

Concorde Hotel

2 Jalan Sultan Ismail; tel: 03-2144 2200; www.concorde.net/kl; $$–$$$

Though one of the older hotels in the city, Concorde has held its own with large and airy rooms. Guests in the Premier Executive wing enjoy a range of services, such as complimentary limousine transfers from the airport, free refreshments at the lounge and a separate reception area.

Crowne Plaza Mutiara

Jalan Sultan Ismail; tel: 03-2148 2322; www.crowneplaza.com; $$$

Sitting on a beautifully landscaped 5-hectare (12-acre) property, this has spacious rooms with large bathrooms and rain showers. Guests in executive club rooms and suites enjoy complimentary breakfast and cocktails.

Hotel Equatorial KL

Jalan Sultan Ismail; tel: 03-2161 7777; www.equatorial.com/kul; $$$

Its functional and comfortable rooms have amenities geared towards business travellers. Its restaurants are among the city's most favoured for high tea and Japanese fare.

Hotel Maya

138 Jalan Ampang; tel: 03-2711 8866; www.hotelmaya.com.my; $$$

This boutique hotel boasts innovative interior design, comfortable beds and huge bathrooms. Its guests-only Sky Lounge provides views of the Twin Towers and KL Tower. Still Waters restaurant serves excellent *sosaku* (creative) Japanese cuisine.

Impiana KLCC Hotel & Spa

13 Jalan Pinang; tel: 03-2147 1111; www.impiana.com/klcc.html; $$

This spa retreat for business travellers offers spacious, modern rooms, a wide choice of therapies at the Swasana Spa and an infinity pool. A walkway connects to the KL Convention Centre.

Mandarin Oriental

Kuala Lumpur City Centre; tel: 03-2380 8888; www.mandarin oriental.com; $$$$

Often touted as a 6-star facility, this has large guest rooms that combine traditional and contemporary furnishings with cutting-edge technology. The ceiling-to-floor windows offer fabulous views of the Twin Towers, and 300-odd original artworks are displayed throughout the hotel. The Thalgo Marine Spa provides a relaxing diversion from the hustle of city life.

Pacific Regency Hotel Apartments

Menara PanGlobal, Jalan Punchak, off Jalan P. Ramlee; tel: 03-2332 7777; www.pacific-regency.com; $$$

Longer-staying tourists will appreciate the serviced apartments opposite the KL Tower. Choose from studios and two-bedroom units, all with fully equipped kitchenettes and free wireless broadband access. Its rooftop Luna Bar is one of the city's top nightspots.

Above from far left: luxurious furnishings at The Ascott; Mandarin Oriental health club.

Prices
Prices quoted are net, inclusive of government and services taxes. Bargain for better rates, especially for longer stays. internet and weekend rates in the city tend to be lower. Buffet breakfast is usually included and airport transfers or tours are sometimes thrown in.

Shangri-La Hotel

11 Jalan Sultan Ismail; tel: 03-2032 2388; www.shangri-la.com/kualalumpur; $$$$

This hotel, located across the pulsating nightclubs of Jalan Sultan Ismail, has lovely gardens, a large gym and capacious rooms. The restaurants are popular at weekends, so book a table if you are dining there. The KL Tower and the lush Bukit Nanas Forest Recreational Park are just behind.

Traders Hotel

Kuala Lumpur City Centre; tel: 03-2332 9888; www.tradershotels.com; $$$

Connected to the KL Convention Centre, this sleek new hotel is popular with business travellers, with five exclusive Traders Club floors. The contemporary-style rooms have full length windows with views of either the city or the Twin Towers.

Lake Gardens, KL Sentral, Brickfields and Mid Valley

Boulevard Hotel

Mid Valley City, Lingkaran Syed Putra; tel: 03-2295 8000; www.blvhotel.com; $$

The Mid Valley area has two enormous malls, so this hotel is great for shoppers. The rooms are large and offer a flat-screen TV and beautiful artworks on the walls. Provides a shuttle to the Bangsar LRT station, and the KTM Komuter train station is within walking distance.

Carcosa Seri Negara

Taman Tasik Perdana, Persiaran Mahameru; tel: 03-2282 1888; www.carcosa.com.my; $$$$

Its suites, housed in two restored colonial mansions with sprawling gardens, have hosted dignitaries from around the world. Some have a terrace; all come with separate dining, dressing and living rooms and 24-hour butler service. Don't miss the afternoon high tea and curry tiffin lunch.

Cititel Hotel

Mid Valley City, Lingkaran Syed Putra; tel: 03-2296 1188; www.cititelhotel.com; $$

After an RM8 million upgrade, Cititel's rooms now sport features catering to business travellers. With shops virtually at your doorstep, you can shop, eat and stroll back to your room any time.

Hilton Kuala Lumpur

3 Jalan Stesen Sentral; tel: 03-2264 2264; www.kuala-lumpur.hilton.com; $$$

The bright rooms have floor-to-ceiling windows with views of the city, luxurious beds, rain showers and large-screen plasma TVs. A free-form pool, a multi-restaurant hub and the Zeta Bar, which has KL's who's who in attendance, add to its appeal.

Price for a double room with breakfast and taxes:	
$$$$	over RM400
$$$	RM300–399
$$	RM100–299
$	below RM100

Le Meridien

2 Jalan Stesen Sentral; tel: 03-2263
7888; www.lemeridien.com; $$$

This swanky establishment located in
the transport hub of KL Sentral comes
with contemporary furnishings, Jim
Thompson silk upholstery, marble
bathrooms and a lovely landscaped
pool area. Rooms have great views.

Jalan Tuanku Abdul Rahman and Surroundings

Coliseum Café & Hotel

98–100 Jalan Tuanku Abdul
Rahman; tel: 03-2692 6270; $

This quaint hotel, which dates back
to the 1920s, once welcomed colonial
characters who frequented the bar and
the restaurant. Today, a mostly back-
packer crowd fills the rooms – doubles
are air-conditioned; singles are fan-
cooled. Its original decor still remains.

Quality Hotel City Centre

Jalan Raja Laut; tel: 03-2693 9233;
www.quality.com.my; $$

This family-friendly place has large
beds and a coffee house serving a good
buffet breakfast. Close to malls such as
Pertama Complex and the Japanese
department store Sogo.

Tune Hotel

316 Jalan Tuanku Abdul Rahman;
tel: 03-7962 5888; www.tune
hotels.com; $

Much like a budget airline (and in fact
linked to AirAsia), this hotel has comfortable beds and luxurious showers but
otherwise few frills. Book early online
to get rates as low as RM9.99 a night.

Bukit Bintang

Bintang Warisan

68 Jalan Bukit Bintang; tel: 03-2148
8111; www.bintangwarisan.com; $$

This 10-storey heritage boutique hotel
is situated just behind the Jalan Alor
hawker stalls. Has clean rooms,
laundry service and airport transfers.

Dorsett Regency Hotel

172 Jalan Imbi; tel: 03-2715 1000;
www.dorsettregency.com.my; $$

A stylish 4-star facility that belies its
bland exterior. Most rooms have good
views of the Twin Towers. The Esquire
Club rooms and packages are great
value with complimentary services such
as airport transfers and internet access.

The Federal

35 Jalan Bukit Bintang; tel: 03-2148
9166; www.federal.com.my; $$

Built in time for the country's 1957
independence celebrations, this city
landmark has a quirky eco-floor with
plastic-free and organic features. Its
revolving restaurant, with panoramic
views, serves fine-dining Western meals.

Grand Millennium

160 Jalan Bukit Bintang; tel: 03-
2117 4888; www.millenniumhotels.
com; $$$$

Tastefully appointed rooms with big
bathtubs complete with nature-based
L'Occitane toiletries. A great location
for shopping, food and entertainment.

The Green Hut Lodge

48 Tengkat Tong Shin; tel: 03-2141
3339; www.thegreenhut.com; $

**Above from far
left:** chic decor
at the Hotel Maya
(see p.111);
Carcosa Seri
Negara's colonial
façade; Cititel Hotel
in Mid Valley City.

Hotel Service
Hotels are rated
1 to 5 stars
according to
international criteria
such as size,
facilities and staff-
to-guest ratio
(see the Malaysian
Association of
Hotels website
at www.hotels.
org.my). However,
other than the
5-star hotels and
backpacker outfits,
service can be
wanting due to
poor training and
the increased
employment of
migrant workers
with a poor
command of
English. Be patient.

Book Early
Rooms can be booked out and a surcharge imposed during peak periods, which are long weekends, Malaysian and Singaporean school holidays in June and December, the Formula 1 Grand Prix season in March, public holidays, especially Chinese New Year and Hari Raya Aidilfitri, and July–August when Arab tourists flock to the country.

This spotless backpacker's accommodation boasts ethnic interiors, bold colours and a well-designed common area that comes alive at night. There are dorms, and twin-share and single rooms. All rooms are air-conditioned and have hot showers.

JW Marriott

183 Jalan Bukit Bintang; tel: 03-2715 9000; www.marriott.com; $$$

This hotel has all the required mod cons for business travellers. It is part of the Starhill Gallery complex, so guests can take advantage of the spa and health facilities in the mall and charge their dining expenses at the Feast Village to their rooms.

Number Eight Guesthouse

8–10 Tengkat Tong Shin; tel: 03-2144 2050; www.numbereight. com.my; $

This friendly accommodation with Straits Chinese decor has dorms, twins, doubles and ensuite rooms. Amenities include air-conditioning or fans, hot showers and free internet access.

The Ritz-Carlton

168 Jalan Imbi; tel: 03-2142 8000; www.ritzcarlton.com/hotels/kuala_lumpur; $$$$

This has one of the city's best personalised butler services, along with charming touches like chilled aromatherapy towels and butler-drawn baths. Indulge in outdoor spa baths and therapies at its Spa Village.

The Westin

199 Jalan Bukit Bintang; tel: 03-2731 8333; www.westin.com/kualalumpur; $$$$

This stylish hotel has large rooms with luxurious beds and bathrooms. Parents will appreciate its Kids Club and baby-sitting services, and party-goers should not miss Qba, a fancy Latin-themed nightspot.

Fraser's Hill

Highland Resthouse Holdings Bungalows

Sales office: Suite 38A-1, 38/F, Empire Tower, City Square Centre, 182 Jalan Tun Razak; tel: 03-2164 8937; www.hrhbungalows.com; $$–$$$$

These renovated colonial bungalows combine contemporary comfort with old-world charm. Complete with dining and living rooms and English-style gardens, its three 3-room and two 4-room bungalows are only available for rent as a whole while the chalets and Pekan Bungalow rooms can be rented individually.

The Smokehouse Hotel & Restaurant

Jalan Jeriau; tel: 09-362 2226; www.thesmokehouse.com.my/fh.htm; $$

Built in 1924, this Tudor-style gem has beautiful stone masonry and mani-

cured gardens. Rooms are cosy, and each one is different, offering either hill or garden views. The public spaces are filled with chintz and memorabilia.

Genting Highlands

Genting Highlands Resort

Tel: 03-2718 1118; www.genting. com.my/en/accommodation; $$–$$$

Choose from six hotels with over 10,000 rooms on Genting Highlands: the 5-star **Genting Hotel** and **Highlands Hotel** (where the casino is); the 4-star **Resort Hotel**; the 3-star **Theme Park Hotel** (where the indoor theme park sits) and **First World Hotel** (said to be the world's largest hotel); and the **Awana Genting Highlands Golf & Country Resort**, set in lovely green surrounds.

Kuala Selangor

Kuala Selangor Nature Park

Jalan Klinik; tel: 03-3289 2294; $

Accommodation options are basic: A-frame huts (twin-share), chalets (triple-share), dorms and a hostel. Amenities include running water, 24-hour electricity and a common kitchen, but not much else. Walk 10 minutes to the old town centre for meals.

Petaling Jaya

Hilton Petaling Jaya

2 Jalan Barat; tel: 03-7955 9122; www.hilton.com; $$

Located just off the Federal Highway, with airy rooms, delicious local cuisine, a popular pub that serves excellent steaks, and a Davidoff cigar store. The gym is good for fitness buffs and the spa next to it does wonders for muscle soreness afterwards.

Shah's Village Hotel

3 & 5 Lorong Sultan, Seksyen 52; tel: 03-7956 9322; www.shahs resorts.com; $$

This family-run hotel has quaint rooms with endearing details such as batik sarongs for guests' use. Boasts a tropical resort feel with swaying palm trees around the swimming pool. The LRT is a short walk away.

Sunway Resort Hotel & Spa

Persiaran Lagoon, Bandar Sunway; tel: 03-7492 8000; www.sunway hotels.com; $$$$

A family-friendly hotel with easy access to the Sunway Lagoon water theme park and Sunway Pyramid shopping mall. The decor is a kitschy Malaysian version of South Africa's famous Palace of the Lost City at Sun City. Avoid rooms just beneath the lobby as it can be noisy overhead.

Putrajaya

Hotel Equatorial Bangi-Putrajaya

Off Persiaran Bandar, Bandar Baru Bangi; tel: 03-8210 2222; www.equatorial.com/bng; $$$$

Built like a Spanish villa, this is majestically perched atop a hill amid lush tropical gardens, and has an expansive 27-hole championship golf course. Offers services including traditional massage and a fitness centre. A shuttle bus goes several times a day to its sister hotel at the heart of KL.

Above from far left: tip of the Grand Millennium; a Sunway Resort villa that comes with a private infinity pool.

Chinese

Chef Choi

159 Jalan Ampang; tel: 03-2163 5866; daily noon–2.30pm and 6–10pm; $$$

Cantonese cuisine with modern twists. Its melt-in-your-mouth steamed fish, the test of excellence in a Chinese restaurant, is divine, as are other favourites such as prawns in Chinese wine and saffron sauce and fragrant duck wrapped in pancakes.

Crystal Jade La Mian Xiao Long Bao

R2 Annexe Block, Lot 10 Shopping Centre, Jalan Sultan Ismail; tel: 03-2148 2338; daily 11am–10.30pm; $$

Brisk service and delicious Shanghainese and northern Chinese dishes. Order the *xiao long bao* (dumplings), which burst with juiciness in every bite, and hand-pulled noodles with pork ribs.

Dain Ti Hill

Lot 6.01.05, 6/F, Pavilion KL, 168 Jalan Bukit Bintang; tel: 03-2145 6628; daily 11am–10pm; $$

The food is as fashionable as the decor of this modern 'Tang dynasty-inspired' eatery. Desserts are listed first in the menu – deservingly so – and comprise delectable offerings like ice-cream and red beans on a warm sweet potato base. Popular main courses include the sautéed beef steak and the sushi-like imperial roll with prawn or eel.

Hakka Restaurant

6 Jalan Kia Peng; tel: 03-2143 1908; daily noon–3pm and 6pm–midnight; $$

This family-run restaurant, over 40 years old, is the best place for authentic Hakka food. Must-tries are the Hakka noodles with minced pork sauce, *mui choy kau yok* (braised pork belly layered with preserved vegetables) and the tender *yim kok kai* (salt-baked chicken).

Hong Ngek Restaurant

50 Jalan Tun H.S. Lee; tel: 03-2078 7852; Mon–Sat 10am–7pm; $

Tuck into deep-fried pork ribs, pomfret in two styles (steamed and deep-fried), and double-boiled winter melon soup. Its Hokkien noodles is also a must – yellow noodles in a sticky dark sauce with pork, seafood and vegetables.

Kedai Kopi Weng Hing

183 Jalan Imbi; daily 7am–midnight; $

More than 30 years old, this coffee shop offers the best pork ball noodles in town, served in soup or tossed in gravy. Try the melt-in-your-mouth *siu yok* (roast pork) and *char siu* (barbecued pork), and also scrumptious bean curd and chicken braised in soy sauce.

The Oriental Bowl

5 & 7 Lebuh Pudu; tel: 03-2032 5577; Mon–Sat 10am–6.30pm; $$

Imbibe nutritious double-boiled soups

Price per person for a three-course meal without drinks:

$$$$	over RM90
$$$	RM60–90
$$	RM30–60
$	below RM30

Above from far left: roast meat and dim sum at a Chinese restaurant; classy setup at La Bodega (see p.48); a wholesome salad.

such as 'Dancing Buddha' – with wild American ginseng, dried scallops and sea cucumber. The tasty soups are made from stock made by simmering the pork bones and chicken for hours.

Restoran Teochew

270–272 Jalan Changkat Thambi Dollah, off Jalan Pudu; tel: 03-2141 4704; daily 7am–3pm and 6pm–midnight; $$

A dim sum place, serving 40 varieties from Monday to Saturday, and a whopping 100 types on Sunday. Try the *yat chan fung*, literally 'a gust of wind', which are baked sticky buns filled with barbecued pork so named because a puff of air gushes out as you take a bite. There are also other Teochew favourites such as braised goose and fish-paste noodles.

Sin Kee Restoran

194 Jalan Tun Sambanthan; tel: 03-2274 1842; Tue–Sun noon–2.30pm and 6–9.30pm; $

Home-style Chinese food. Order a few dishes to share: *sambal* (chilli paste) prawns, fresh seafood steamed with rice, *fu yung*-style omelette with Chinese sausage, prawns and onions. Hainanese-style one-dish 'Western' meals such as fish and chips, and lamb and chicken chops are available too.

Sun Hong Muk Koot Teh

35, 37, 39 & 41 Medan Imbi; tel: 03-2141 4064; daily 5am–midnight; $

A good stop for *bak kut teh*, a hearty herbal broth with pork ribs, entrails and bean curd puffs, eaten with *you tiao*

(Chinese crullers) and yam rice. Try the sweet-sourish pig's trotters in black vinegar and chicken in rice wine too.

French

Le Bouchon

14 & 16 Changkat Bukit Bintang; tel: 03-2142 7633; Tue–Fri noon–2pm and 7–10.30pm, Sat–Sun 7–10.30pm; $$$

You'll think you've stepped into a little rustic French country house when you dine here. Enjoy garlic and spinach escargots, goose liver terrine, braised ox tongue with gherkins, mushrooms and Madeira sauce, and grilled rack of lamb provencale.

Frangipani

25 Changkat Bukit Bintang; tel: 03-2144 3001; Tue–Sun 7.30–10.30pm; $$$$

This chic French fine-dining outlet, with tables set around a pool, offers a lovely intimate atmosphere. Must-haves are the tea-smoked salmon with coffee-flavoured mash, roasted duck confit with mustard cream, and its signature dessert – chocolate ganache with candied almond meringue. Excellent wine collection.

Ma Maison

32 Persiaran Ampang; tel: 03-4256 5410; Wed–Mon noon–3pm and 6.30–10pm; $ (set lunch), $$$ (à la carte), cash only

Classic French cuisine in this restaurant furnished like a cosy house. Excellent set lunch: appetiser buffet with salads, pâté and breads, with a

Cutlery, Please?
Chopsticks are used in Chinese eateries, but you could ask for a plate and cutlery, which translates in Malaysia to a fork and spoon, no knives. Patrons of the smaller and more traditional Malay and Indian eateries often use their hands to eat but again, forks and spoons are available too.

choice of three mains that change daily. For dinner, there is the *escalope de foie gras Miss Chan*, named after a regular diner, and the grilled duck breast with green pepper sauce.

German

Deutsches Haus

46 Changkat Bukit Bintang; tel: 03-2143 2268; daily 3pm–midnight; $$$

This wood-clad, pub-like country German restaurant dishes up hearty platters of home-made pork sausages and a superb pork knuckle, which you can wash down with a range of German lagers. Popular with expats.

Karl's Beisl

Lobby, Bangsar Puteri Condo, Jalan Medang Serai; tel: 03-2094 0628; Tue–Sun 11am–10pm; $$

Austrian country-style home cooking. Chef Karl Rathswohl offers *bratwurst*, suckling pig and stuffed beef roulade. A collector too, he presents much more for your eyes – antique chairs, an Egyptian gold mirror and a Black Forest clock. Great place for afternoon tea with scones and pastries.

Indian

B'Sentral

50 Jalan Vivekananda, off Jalan Tun Sambantan, Brickfields; tel: 03-2278 8646; daily 8am–3am; $

South Indian variations such as claypot *biryani* (chicken, mutton or seafood) and dory fish with an unmistakable Indian garlic-and-chilli flavour. The floor is artistically decorated with wooden sleepers salvaged from railway

tracks. Sports bar upstairs, with pool tables, televised sports and beer.

Gem Restaurant

124 Jalan Tun Sambanthan, Brickfields; tel: 03-2260 1373; daily 11am–3pm and 6–11pm; $$

Tandoori fans will like Gem's special tandoor sizzling platter comprising fish tikka, tandoori chicken, *murgh badami* kebab (chicken kebab) and *seekh* kebab (mutton kebab). For vegetarians, Gem has a *thali* rice set, and the smooth *palak paneer* (mashed spinach with goat cheese). Jain food (no onions or garlic) is also available.

Lotus Family Restaurant

79 Lebuh Ampang; tel: 03-2026 1689; daily 7am–10pm; $

South Indian cuisine. A wide variety of sides – chicken curry, *sambal* (chilli) prawns and more, to go with your *biryani* rice set with *pappadam* (spicy lentil wafers) and *rasam* (lentil gravy). Savoury snacks – samosas, curry puffs, onion *pakora* (fritters) and dhal patties – are served for tea.

Passage Through India

4 Jalan Delima, off Bukit Bintang; tel: 03-2145 0366; daily noon–2.30pm and 6.30–11pm; $$

Price per person for a three-course meal without drinks:

$$$$	over RM90
$$$	RM60–90
$$	RM30–60
$	below RM30

Housed in an old bungalow, this North Indian restaurant scores for atmosphere and a menu that covers the range from Goan seafood to meats from Assam. Try its *dum biryani* (a spicy rice and meat dish), divine fish tikka and excellent prawn *jalfrazi* (dry curry).

Restoran Ahamedia

18 Medan Pasar; tel: 03-2031 3982; daily 6.30am–10.30pm; $

Dine on tandoor-baked *naan* bread and lentil curry while gazing at the historical Masjid Jamek. Try also its Indian breads like *roti canai* (flaky bread), *chapati* (flat bread) and *thosai* (a paper-thin rice flour pancake). The moist and fragrant *nasi biryani* (rice cooked with spices and ghee) is delicious when topped with chicken curry.

Sithique Nasi Kandar Pulau Pinang

233 Jalan Tuanku Abdul Rahman; tel: 016-382 4867; daily 7am–7.30pm; $

It is Penang-style curry galore here. Choose from fish head, squid, beef, lamb and other curries, to be splashed over rice or to go with Indian breads like *roti canai* (flaky bread) and *thosai* (a paper-thin rice flour pancake).

International

Fisherman's Cove

LG10, Feast Floor, Starhill Gallery, 181 Jalan Bukit Bintang; tel: 03-2782 3848; daily noon–1am; $$$$

Savour fresh seafood in a 'boathouse', with sails for walls and bamboo structures on an upper deck. Start with a seafood soup, move on to steamed organic barramundi or pan-seared scallops cooked in a sauce that includes sea urchin, and end with the sinful ivory chocolate and warm soufflé with orange ice cream.

Mezza Notte Italian Restaurant and Sushi Bar

The Loft, 28–40 Asian Heritage Row, Jalan Doraisamy; tel: 03-2691 5667; Mon–Sat noon–2.30pm and 6.30–10.30pm, Fri–Sat till 11pm; $$

An unusual union of Italian and Japanese cuisines – from sushi to traditional Italian desserts – is served here. This swanky restaurant's concept has proven to be so popular that bookings are imperative on weekends.

Restaurant Lafite

Shangri-La Hotel, 11 Jalan Sultan Ismail; tel: 03-2074 3900; Mon–Fri noon–2.30pm, Mon–Sat 7–10.30pm; $$$$

Award-winning chef Kevin Cherkas, formerly of Spain's El Bulli, adopts new methods and technology in food preparation; in short, molecular gastronomy. Diners will be pleasantly surprised by the lobster thermidor and seared lamb with sautéed vegetables.

Saffron

Pavilion 2, One Bangsar, 63G Jalan Ara, Bangsar Baru; tel: 03-2287 1158; Mon–Sat 11am–3pm, 7–11pm; $$ (set lunch), $$$$ (à la carte)

This fine-dining outlet's 200-strong menu items are a mix of Mediter-

ranean and Middle Eastern. Popular tapas include *champinones al ajilio* (sautéed butter mushrooms in olive oil with garlic, parsley and butter) and *gambas al ajilio* (sautéed tiger prawns in olive oil with garlic and parsley). Meat lovers have grills, steaks and seafood to choose from, while salads and pastas cater to vegetarians.

Italian

Santini

Lot G458, G/F, Suria KLCC; tel: 03-2382 0329; daily 11am–midnight; $$
Highly recommended bistro with a view of the buzzing KLCC Park. Start with a beef carpaccio or garlic escargot, and move on to the *gnocchi* with gorgonzola cheese or seafood paella served in a cast-iron pan. End with the delightful almond tiramisu.

Japanese

Kampachi

Hotel Equatorial, Jalan Sultan Ismail; tel: 03-2161 7777; daily noon–2.30pm and 6.30–11pm; $$$
Thirty years on and it is still the finest Japanese restaurant in the city, with a wine cellar and a sushi counter. Excellent soft-shell crab *maki* (rolled sushi), beef *sukiyaki* (hotpot) and grilled *unagi* (eel). Attracts a discerning

> Price per person for a three-course meal without drinks:
>
> | | |
> |---|---|
> | $$$$ | over RM90 |
> | $$$ | RM60–90 |
> | $$ | RM30–60 |
> | $ | below RM30 |

crowd especially for its Sunday brunch and Saturday semi-buffet.

Mizu Japanese Fine Dining

1/F, Bangsar Village; tel: 03-2283 6988; Mon–Fri noon–3pm and 6–10.30pm, Sat–Sun noon–10.30pm; $$$
Minimalist decor and jazz music create a relaxed mood at this chic restaurant. Inspired by cosmopolitan Tokyo, the chefs dish up the freshest sashimi; other must-tries are the *chawanmushi* (steamed egg) with foie gras, salmon cheese *maki* and tempura oyster with cheese. Impressive wine and sake lists.

Still Waters

Hotel Maya, 138 Jalan Ampang; tel: 03-2711 8866; daily noon–2.30pm and 6.30–10.30pm; $$ (set lunch), $$$ (à la carte)
Exquisite *sosaku* (creative) cuisine, combining Japanese and Western ingredients in delicate dishes such as lamb truffle, gratin scallops, miso cod fish and beef wasabi. Water features surround you as you dine in this cosy, modern eatery.

Korean

Koryo Won

Lot 19, 2/F, Kompleks Antarabangsa, Jalan Sultan Ismail; tel: 03-2142 7655; daily noon–2.30pm and 5.30–10.30pm; $$$
The aroma of meat being grilled in front of you makes this eatery's barbecued beef and spare ribs irresistible. Accompany your choice with *kimchi* (pickled vegetables), tofu and spicy

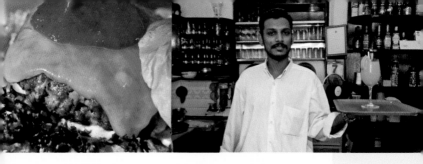

cockles. Other goodies are *samk yeh tang* (double-boiled chicken soup with ginseng and glutinous rice) and *dolsot bab* (boiled red rice in stone pot).

Above from far left: spicy Malay cuisine; Chinoz on the Park *(see p.40)*; gourmet burger at Relish *(see p.62)*; Coliseum Café bartender *(see p.58)*.

Malay

Bijan Restaurant

3 Jalan Ceylon; tel: 03-2031 3575; daily 11.30am–2.30pm and 6.30–10.30pm; $ (set lunch), $$ (à la carte).

Bijan's contemporary interior welcomes with lots of wood, bamboo and colourful batik art. Sumptuous Malay cuisine; try *masak lemak udang tempoyak* (prawns in fermented durian curry – seasonal), char-grilled short beef ribs with *sambal* (chilli paste) and *kerabu pucuk paku* (jungle fern salad).

CT Rose

Jalan Datuk Abdul Razak (opposite Sekolah Kebangsaan Kampung Baru), Kampung Baru; tel: 016-997 8701; daily 6.30pm–5.30am; $

The biggest *nasi lemak* stall in the city has a stunning view of the Twin Towers. Locals come to get their fix of coconut rice cooked in giant pots. More pots are filled with different *sambal* (chilli paste) of anchovies, squid, beef *rendang* and chicken curry.

Satay Kajang Hj Samuri

No. 79, Jalan 21/37, Damansara Uptown, Petaling Jaya; tel: 03-7710 5318; Sat–Thur 11am–midnight, Fri 3pm–midnight; $

Superbly marinated, tender to the bite and accompanied by a smooth peanut sauce, this has the best Malaysian *satay*.

Malaysian

Bayu Timor

KS01, 2/F, Sungei Wang Plaza, Jalan Sultan Ismail; tel: 03-2143 1205; daily 9.30am–9pm; $

Dine amidst teak furniture and bric-a-brac in this charming café that offers the city's best *mee siam*, vermicelli in a hot-and-sour gravy with prawns, chicken and egg; it sells out quickly, so get there early. Other specials are the coconut and curried Sarawak *laksa* and Penang *rojak* (spicy fruit salad).

Kedai Ayam Panggang Wong Ah Wah

1, 3, 5, 7 & 9 Jalan Alor, off Jalan Bukit Bintang; tel: 03-2144 2463; daily 5pm–3.45am, closed alternate Mon; $

Local street food at its best here, down a bustling lane. Grilled chicken wings are the main draw, but equally lip-smacking are the grilled fish, oyster omelette, crabs in a salted egg sauce, and chilli-fried cockles. There is also a wide range of Cantonese dishes.

Little Penang Kafe

Lot 409–411, 4/F, Suria KLCC; tel: 03-2163 0215; daily 11.30am–3.30pm and 4.30–9.30pm; $

Serves dishes from the island of Penang, well known as a gourmet's paradise. Try its *char kway teow* (fried flat rice noodles), hot and sour *asam laksa* with a spicy tamarind fish gravy, and Hokkien prawn noodles. For dessert, order *ice kacang*, a sweet shaved ice treat. Another branch at Mid Valley Megamall (tel: 03-2282 0215).

Hawker Fare
Locals will swear that hawker food is the best food on earth. How to choose what to eat? Read up about it or ask locals, be adventurous and just follow the crowd and order from stalls that attract the most custom. Hawker stall dining, whether in a *kopitiam* (coffee shop) or exposed to the elements on a roadside kerb, is an experience in itself.

Paya Serai

Hilton Petaling Jaya, 2 Jalan Barat, Petaling Jaya; tel: 03-7955 9122; daily 6am–2.30am; $$

Popular eatery offering *kampung* (village)-style Malay fare like *ayam kari kandar* (chicken curry) to go with the rice cake (*ketupat daun palas)* and fresh *kerabu* salads. Chinese favourites include braised duck and deep-fried fish with Thai sauce while the Indian mutton *masala* gets high scores. Alternatively, time it right to enjoy its local high tea goodies, an absolute treat.

Yut Kee

35 Jalan Dang Wangi; tel: 03-2698 8108; Tue–Sun 7.45am–6pm; $

A Hainanese coffee shop dating from the 1920s, well known for *roti babi*, a sandwich filled with minced pork and crabmeat, dipped in egg and then deep-fried, served with Worcestershire sauce. Not to be missed too are the *asam* (tamarind) prawns, *belacan* (shrimp paste) fried rice and beef tripe stew.

Middle Eastern

Restoran Tarbush

138 Jalan Bukit Bintang; tel: 03-2142 8558; daily 11am–1.30am; $$

Fine Middle Eastern cuisine in a casual restaurant that is warmly lit by filigree lamps. Begin with excellent starters like the hummus and *baba ghanoush* (eggplant dip) before enjoying the Tarbush mixed grill of chicken, *shish* kebab, lamb cubes and chops. Other outlets at Suria KLCC food court and Starhill Gallery.

Nonya

Precious Old China Restaurant & Bar

Lot 2, Mezzanine Floor, Central Market, Jalan Hang Kasturi; tel: 03-2273 7372; daily 11.30am–9.30pm; $$

Eclectically decorated with Victorian furniture and antique Chinese wall panels, this restaurant's real draws are its chicken cooked *pongteh* or devilled style, omelette with *cincalok* (fermented prawns), and the fried *asam* prawns and *lemak nenas* squid. End with a creamy *bubur cha-cha* dessert.

Top Hat Restaurant

7 Jalan Kia Peng; tel: 03-2141 8611; daily noon–midnight; $$$

Old angsana trees and heliconia plants lend an old-world charm to this restaurant set in an elegant bungalow. The menu features favourites like 'top hats' – pastry cups filled with vegetables and meat, *laksa* noodles and coconut-laced curries. Their Western menu features delicate Asian twists.

Thai

Basil Leaf

35 Jalan Damai, off Jalan Tun Razak; tel: 03-2166 1689; daily noon–2.30pm and 6.30–10.30pm; $$$$

> Price per person for a three-course meal without drinks:
>
> $$$$ over RM90
> $$$ RM60–90
> $$ RM30–60
> $ below RM30

A gorgeous alfresco setting for the romantics at heart. Specials include steamed mixed seafood served in a coconut, a lovely *tom yam* soup, grilled beef in Laotian sauce and the tangy Vietnamese prawn and mango salad. Wines and other alcoholic drinks are available, otherwise the lemon grass drink is delightfully refreshing.

Basil Thai Nudle Bar

G10, G/F, Bangsar Village, 1 Jalan Telawi 1; tel: 03-2287 8708; daily noon–10pm; $

Casual café with a menu of traditional Thai dishes. The special mix combo platter, with spring rolls, *wan tons* and fish cakes, is an appetite-whetting starter. For mains, order the prawn *tom yam* (hot and sour soup), green curry or stir-fried beef with basil.

Vegetarian

Dharma Realm Guan Yin Sagely Monastery

161 Jalan Ampang; tel: 03-2164 8055; Mon–Fri 11am–4pm; $

Queue up with other vegans for a Chinese 'Buddhist' buffet in the simple canteen of the monastery. The canteen serves a large variety of hot food, salads and fruit. Meals are served free on the auspicious 1st and 15th days of the month of the lunar calendar.

Karuna's Restaurant

235 Jalan Tun Sambathan, Brickfields; tel: 03-2273 0100; daily 7am–7.30pm; $

This lacto-vegetarian- and vegan-friendly South Indian restaurant has a good lunch buffet. Alternatively, order a rice-and-curry *thali* set; try the mock meat dishes. The food has no MSG.

Yin Futt Kuok

52 Jalan Hang Lekir; tel: 03-2070 7468; daily 10am–8pm; $

Popular restaurant serving vegetarian fare. Dishes like *asam* 'fish' in a spicy tamarind soup, 'prawns' on hot plate, and sweet and sour 'pork' are prepared with gluten and bean curd sheets. Don't miss out on lovely pastries like 'Wife's Biscuits' *(loh por pheng)* and almond biscuits.

Vietnamese

Bongsen

Lot 416, 4/F, Suria KLCC; tel: 03-2164 6313; daily 11.30am–9.30pm; $$$

This slick French-Vietnamese restaurant offers a platter of assorted appetisers like rolls and prawn dumplings. For the main course, the chefs whip up a traditional *pho bo* (beef noodles) or the spicier Hue variation, *bun bo Hue*.

Sao Nam Restaurant

25 Tengkat Tong Shin; tel: 03-2144 1225; Tue–Sun 12.30–2.30pm and 7.30–10pm; $$$

Sao Nam's mangosteen and prawn salad, tangy and creamy, is a must-order, as are the roasted boneless duck in a sweet tamarind sauce and the pepper leaf-wrapped grilled beef *la lot*. Sip on a fine wine while you take in the American-Vietnamese pop art on the walls.

Above from far left: whipping up Nonya favourites at Precious Old China; international fare at Shook! *(see p.61)*; pastry shop at Suria KLCC; an intimate and cosy café.

Tea Time
Local names are used when ordering tea and coffee. For example, *teh* (tea) is tea with milk and sugar, *teh o* is black tea with sugar, *teh see* (tea and evaporated milk), and *teh o kosong* (black tea without sugar). The same applies to coffee; thus: *kopi, kopi o, kopi see* and *kopi o kosong*. Note that condensed milk is used instead of fresh milk.

CREDITS

Insight Step by Step Kuala Lumpur
Written by: SL Wong
Proofread and indexed by: Jocelyn Lau
Edited by: Low Jat Leng
Layout by: Derrick Lim
Series Editor: Clare Peel
Cartography Editor: Zoë Goodwin
Picture Manager: Steven Lawrence
Art Editor: Ian Spick
Production: Kenneth Chan
Photography by: Apa: Jon Santa Cruz and Nikt Wong except: The Ascott Kuala Lumpur 110; Bazuki Muhammad/Reuters/Corbis 23T; Carcosa Seri Negara 94CTL, 112–13; Cititel Mid Valley 113TR; Grand Millennium Kuala Lumpur 114; Hotel Maya 112TL; H. Berbar/HBL Network 13B, 23B, 91; HBL Network 65B, 89T; Mandarin Oriental 111; Muzium Negara, Malaysia 22T; Nikt Wong 18C, 30–1, 77T, 80TL, 92; Private Archives 22L; Sunway Resort Hotel & Spa 115; V. Couarraze/HBL Network 90T.
Front Cover: 4Corners (top); Nikt Wong (bottom left); iStockPhoto (bottom right).
Printed by: Insight Print Services (Pte) Ltd, 38 Joo Koon Road, Singapore 628990

www.insightguides.com

DISTRIBUTION

Worldwide
Apa Publications GmbH & Co. Verlag KG (Singapore branch)
38 Joo Koon Road,
Singapore 628990
Tel: (65) 6865 1600
Fax: (65) 6861 6438

UK and Ireland
GeoCenter International Ltd
Meridian House, Churchill Way West,
Basingstoke, Hampshire, RG21 6YR
Tel: (44) 01256 817 987
Fax: (44) 01256 817 988

United States
Langenscheidt Publishers, Inc.
36–36 33rd Street, 4th Floor,
Long Island City, NY 11106
Tel: (1) 718 784 0055
Fax: (1) 718 784 0640

Australia
Universal Publishers
1 Waterloo Road, Macquarie Park, NSW 2113
Tel: (61) 2 9857 3700
Fax: (61) 2 9888 9074

New Zealand
Hema Maps New Zealand Ltd (HNZ)
Unit D, 24 Ra ORA Drive,
East Tamaki, Auckland
Tel: (64) 9 273 6459
Fax: (64) 9 273 6479

CONTACTING THE EDITORS

We would appreciate it if readers would alert us to errors or outdated information by writing to us at insight@apaguide.co.uk or Apa Publications, PO Box 7910, London SE1 1WE, UK.

INDEX

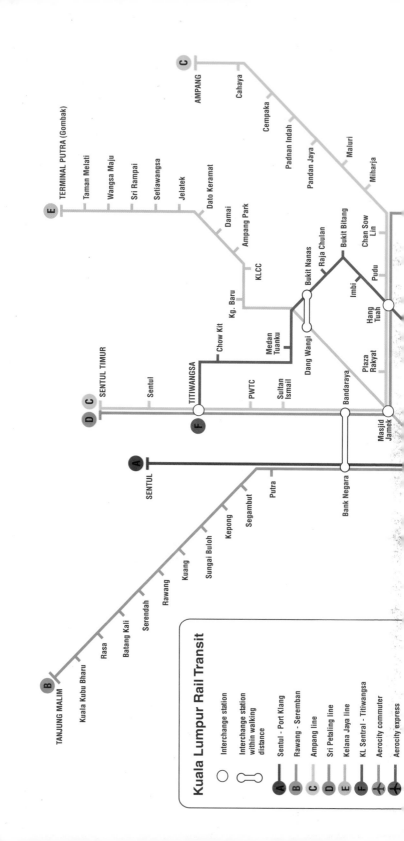

Kuala Lumpur Rail Transit

- ◯ Interchange station
- ⬡ Interchange station within walking distance
- Ⓐ Sentul - Port Klang
- Ⓑ Rawang - Seremban
- Ⓒ Ampang line
- Ⓓ Sri Petaling line
- Ⓔ Kelana Jaya line
- Ⓕ KL Sentral - Titiwangsa
- ✈ Aerocity commuter
- ✈ Aerocity express